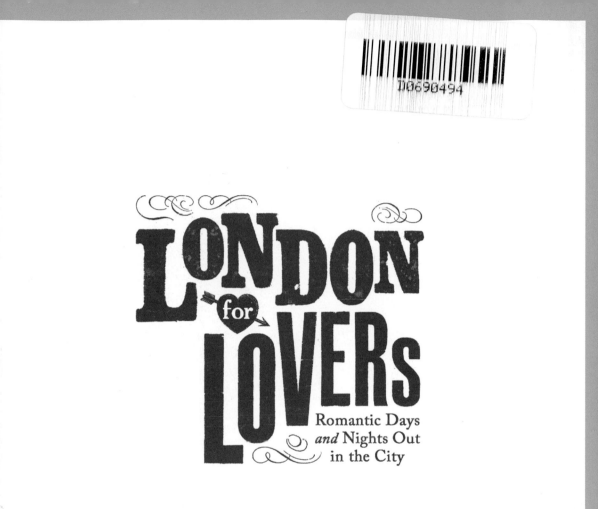

LONDON for LOVERS

Romantic Days
and Nights Out
in the City

LONDON for LOVERS

by SAM HODGES & SOPHIE VICKERS

Romantic Days *and* Nights Out in the City

SQUARE PEG

Published by Square Peg 2013

2 4 6 8 10 9 7 5 3 1

Creative direction by Kristen Harrison at The Curved House
Designed by Rowan Powell at The Curved House
Letterpress artwork by Aardvark Printmongers

First published in Great Britain in 2013 by Square Peg
Random House, 20 Vauxhall Bridge Road, London SW1V 2SA
www.vintage-books.co.uk
Addresses for companies within The Random House Group Limited can be found at:
www.randomhouse.co.uk/offices.htm
The Random House Group Limited Reg. No. 954009
A CIP catalogue record for this book is available from the British Library

ISBN 9780224095525

The Random House Group Limited supports The Forest Stewardship Council (FSC®), the leading
international forest certification organisation. Our books carrying the FSC® label are printed on
FSC®-certified paper. FSC® is the only forest certification scheme endorsed by the leading
environmental organisations, including Greenpeace. Our paper procurement policy
can be found at www.randomhouse.co.uk/environment

Printed and bound in Italy by Graphicom Srl

CONTENTS

••

LEAFY LONDON

LATE-NIGHT LONDON

LAST-MINUTE LONDON

LAZY LONDON

LEARNED LONDON

LIVE LONDON

LEFT-FIELD LONDON

LOST LONDON

Hampstead

Highgate Cemetry

King's Cross

Kensal Rise

Primrose Hill

Isling

Regents Park

Queen's Park

Lincon's Inn Fi

The Seven Noses of Soho

Kensington Gardens

Notting Hill

Aldwyc

Shepherd Market

Somerset H

St James's Park

Chelsea

River Thames

Brixton

Richmond Park &
Twickenham

N
W E
S

Hackney Wick

Dalston

Columbia Road

Shoreditch

Spitalfield's

Brick Lane

The City of London

Wapping

th Bank

Bermondsey

Greenwich

Crystal Palace

Dulwich

Forest Hill

LEAFY

LONDON

FROM SWAINS LANE ACROSS HAMPSTEAD HEATH

. . . .

Hampstead

Nicknamed 'Lover's Lane', Hampstead Heath has been a Mecca for romance, inspiration and, indeed, sex for centuries. Described by Wilkie Collins in *The Woman in White* as a 'suburban Nirvana', the Heath is the place for wilfully losing oneself. Its untamed wildness, dissected by long, looping pathways, hides countless surprises for the inquisitive.

Your day of dreamy wanderings begins at **Kalendar Café**, on Swains Lane, just round the corner from the east side of the park, for eggs Benedict and a Konditor & Cook cake to take away. Entering the park past kids on tennis courts and grandpas on bowling lawns, it's worth catching the **Parliament Hill Farmers' Market** (open Saturdays, 10 til 2), where organic produce and stall names (like Giggly Pig Company and Wobbly Bottom Farm) delight in equal measure. If you want to forage for your supper on the Heath, booking ahead is essential for the four-hour **Spring Fungi Foray**, which offers Barboured adventurers the chance to search out the elusive 'Hen of the Woods' and the 'Charcoal Burner'.

Head skywards and emerge, breathless and elated, atop Parliament Hill, also known as 'Kite Hill'. Joggers snatching a breath and children tangled in kite-strings surround the smattering of benches that overlook the spectacular skyline: the skyscrapers of Canary Wharf and the City of London, the pregnant dome of St Paul's Cathedral, the unmistakeably phallic Gherkin, and the Shard, now the tallest building in the EU. The view is surely at its most romantic at twilight, as the lights of the city flicker on one by one – ironically the very spot where Guy

Fawkes' followers assembled to watch Parliament burn (hence the name).

Down the other side of Parliament Hill, the placid **Hampstead Ponds** are an invigorating diversion on a summer's day: the water lilies at the Women's Pond make it the most idyllic, the Men's Pond is more Soho-on-Sea, but the Mixed Ponds are the only areas you can wild-swim together. The nearby lawns were immortalised by Ewan McGregor in *Scenes of a Sexual Nature* and in the 1990 adaptation of the Stephen King novel *It*. Floating in the murky, ice-cold water, a flash of green overhead announces the now famous rose-ringed parakeets – rumour has it that a handful of them were released from the 1951 film set of *The African Queen* at Shepperton Studios in Surrey, but it may also have been escapee pets in Victorian times that started the now ebullient colony. These new pretenders preside over the indigenous residents, which include kingfishers, jackdaws, pipistrelles (the largest colony in London), Daubenton's bats, and, on foot, muntjac deer, foxes, rabbits, terrapins and frogs.

It's an uphill amble, past long grasses in spring and blackberry hedgerows in autumn, to **Kenwood House**, for tea and fruit cake in the sun-dappled courtyard of the Brewhouse Café, housed in an old stable block. Inside Kenwood there's one of the finest – and free – picture collections in London, but in the summer, the main attraction is outside, down the grassy banks, past flowering rhododendrons to a pair of deckchairs for one of **Kenwood's Lakeside Concerts**, an institution that's been going since 1951. Gatecrashers with picnics line the hillside – they may not be able to see the concert, but they can hear it for free.

A hidden wonder of the Heath is the **Pergola and Hill Garden** that overlooks West Heath. The Pergola was dreamt up by Lord Leverhulme in 1904 as a striking setting for garden parties, for which the large gardens of the Hill needed to be considerably raised. As chance would have it, the Hampstead extension to the Northern Line was currently being built so he was able to arrange delivery of wagon-loads of soil and even get paid for his trouble.

In Hampstead itself, minutes from the edge of the park nearest the Ponds, the **Wells Pub** offers salt beef with latkes and a Scrabble board. Just outside, Keats' Bench was, reportedly, where the poet was spotted ill with consumption in 1818, 'sobbing his dying breath into a handkerchief'. Romantic, sort of. And if the romance of *Endymion* hasn't got the blood pumping, then there's always a late-night dash across the park, galvanised by the fear of Dick Turpin's ghost, as he and other 'gentlemen of the road' gallop their way across the Heath on silent hooves.

BENCH MARKS

There are 450 commemorative benches on the Heath, a tradition which is only just over sixty years old. On your Heath ramble you might stumble across some of these inscriptions …

The bench that commemorates the renowned TV scriptwriter Lewis Greifer reads, 'They could do with a bench here.' For the last fifteen years of his life Lewis had a bad leg and lungs, and couldn't walk very far without sitting and resting. On walks near Kenwood, the family would often hear him say, as he stood leaning on his cane, catching his breath, 'They could do with a bench here', 'a sotto voce suggestion to the Parks Authority,' as his son Josh put it.

Each inscription tells a story: 'Ethel Copeland Campbell 1897–1987, Vegetarian, Socialist, Pacifist'; 'Gid and Maurice the armchair philosophers.' Some take a poetic line: 'I was born tomorrow, today I live, yesterday killed me,' Parviz Owsia, Iranian writer. Others are more humorous in tone: 'I don't do walks, please be seated,' implores one, near Kenwood House, alongside the deceased's name, and Barry John Stuart Taylor, in the copse up from Highgate Ponds, is 'Remembered with love for his enthusiasm, contagious laughter … and huge appetite.'

Then there are the ambiguous and therefore intriguing: 'Now in years bestride my eighties, this elysian seat I have vacated, but gentle neighbour sigh not yet, I've only moved to Somerset.' Another, up towards Highgate, whispers: 'She (simply) ran out of time.'

FROM FAIRY TALES TO FLAMINGOES

. . . .

Kensington Gardens

Standing on the ledge he could see trees far away, which were doubtless the Kensington Gardens, and the moment he saw them he entirely forgot that he was now a little boy in a nightgown, and away he flew, right over the houses into the Gardens.

J. M. Barrie, *Peter Pan*

The Italian Gardens, at the Queen Anne's Alcove entrance to the park, mark a triumphant beginning to this walk, with its cluster of classical sculptures and fountains, particularly if you happen to be walking past as they spring to life for the first time each day. It's unlikely that the nineteenth-century architects of the now restored Tazza Fountain at the Long Water end of the gardens could have predicted the culmination of an epic water fight between Colin Firth's Mark Darcy and Hugh Grant's Daniel Cleaver in *Bridget Jones: The Edge of Reason*.

The south side of Long Water lake heralds a much more contemporary fountain, the Diana Memorial Fountain and, a little further on, overlooking the water but deliberately hidden among foliage, is the Peter Pan statue (see **Forever Young**, p23), commissioned by the classic tale's author and local resident, J. M. Barrie. To the right, the Kensington Gardens themselves stretch off into the distance; once the private gardens of Kensington Palace, the landscaping is formal but was still the inspiration for Britpop band Blur's iconic track 'Parklife'.

The Serpentine lake takes over from the Long Water at the Serpentine

Bridge, which also marks the walkway between Kensington Gardens and Hyde Park. From the bridge, the view to the west takes in the entire lake, often covered in a layer of mist, stretching out into the distance. The lake takes its name from the way it snakes through the park; the painter Hogarth took the concept further, writing about 'the serpentine line of beauty', a comment on how the curves of the lake commune with the landscape. In a landscaping fashion not uncommon throughout the country, the lake was originally formed from a series of medieval fish ponds, with the far end dammed up to create a lake.

The lake welcomes all creatures of habit to its waters, from the royal swans, whose mating courtship dance, with necks entwined, is a familiar sight, to the early-morning swimmers in the **lido**, which is open all year. A perk of showing such commitment is the option to join one of the park's more idiosyncratic traditions: the 100-yard swimming competition every Christmas morning at 9 am, a race that has been going since 1864, and whose winner is given the Peter Pan Cup, originally awarded in 1904 by Barrie himself. For the less intrepid, rowing boats are available to hire, although lovers are advised to beware the ghost of Harriet Westbrook, the pregnant wife of poet Percy Bysshe Shelley, found drowned in the lake in December 1816. Not one to hang about, Shelley married Mary

Wollstonecraft Godwin less than two weeks later.

The world-famous **Serpentine Gallery** is the place for a tryst, as indeed it was for Helena Bonham-Carter's Kate Croy and her lover in the film adaptation of Henry James's novel *The Wings of the Dove*. Its 1930s tea-house exterior hides a collection of large rooms bathed in natural light from the gallery's huge windows. The sculptures that pose in multifarious forms about the space could be a retrospective of giants like Louise Bourgeois or a career-establishing showcase for the likes of Damien Hirst, and all exhibitions are free of charge. Each summer sees another renowned architect turn curator with a seasonal pavilion of film screenings, talks and the BBC Proms, while year-round the gallery hosts seminars every Saturday with prominent artists and academics.

The western end of the park boasts **Kensington Palace**, now reopened after a £12 million restoration project, and the new home for Britain's latest celebrity royal couple, William and Kate. But it's past residents that are the main event, with stories from Queen Victoria's life told in her own words in the new Victoria Revealed exhibition and a display of Princess Diana's dresses, billed as 'glimpses of a modern princess'.

On the other side of Kensington Gardens stands one of Queen Victoria's many impressive contributions to London's architectural landscape, the **Albert Memorial**, commissioned in honour of her husband, who died of typhoid at the age of 41. A competition was held to choose the design of the memorial, with seven eminent architects challenged with the same brief, and it was the Gothic Revival effort of George Gilbert Scott that was handed the prize.

If the Palace has left you feeling flush, the **Kensington Roof Gardens** features Sir Richard Branson's brasserie and night club amid three themed gardens sprawling over 1.5 acres – the Spanish Garden, the rose-filled Tudor Garden and the English Woodland, overseen by the four resident flamingoes, Bill, Ben, Splosh and Pecks. As if that doesn't already set it apart, this is all 100 feet above Kensington High Street.

FOREVER YOUNG

A little-known fact about the famous children's story by J. M. Barrie is that its full title is *Peter Pan in Kensington Gardens*. Barrie was fascinated by 'lock-out time', the time at the end of the day when, behind the locked park gates, fairies and other magical creatures could emerge and roam about freely, hidden from the prying eyes of the public.

As made famous in the film *Finding Neverland*, Barrie's inspiration for the character of Peter Pan came from his relationship with the Llewelyn Davies family, whom he would watch in the gardens, while walking his dog Porthos. He began to dream up the idea of a Peter Pan sculpture, for which he took a series of photos of the six-year-old Michael Llewelyn Davies, posing in a specially constructed costume.

His great plan was that the statue would emerge, as if by the very magic that his stories relied upon, for the enchantment of the local children. He paid a sculptor to create and mount the statue in the middle of the night, and then placed a mysterious announcement in *The Times* – 'There is a surprise in store for the children who go to Kensington Gardens to feed the ducks in the Serpentine this morning'. Some locals weren't sure if an author should be allowed to raise a statue in a public park to promote his own work; Barrie himself was unhappy with the likeness and complained that it didn't show the 'devil in the boy', perhaps as Michael wasn't used as the model in the end. But the general reaction was and has remained one of quiet pleasure to all who happen upon it.

FROM THE ISABELLA PLANTATION TO PETERSHAM NURSERIES

· ·

Richmond Park

If there was ever an excuse to stop and 'take in the view', this is it. This particular vista of **Terrace Gardens**, on the right side of Terrace Walk on the way up Richmond Hill towards the park, is so spectacular that it is the only view to have been protected by an Act of Parliament. Sir Walter Scott described it as 'an unrivalled landscape', and J.M.W. Turner immortalised it in his paintings.

But such attention comes at a price, and not a small one. Nearby Downe House used to belong to Mick Jagger and Jerry Hall; Ronnie Wood lived in the house that the actor John Mills used to own, and The Who's Pete Townshend lives at the top of Richmond Hill. While these musical legends overlooked the park, others sit within it. The late British singer Ian Dury has a 'musical bench' that marks his favourite viewing spot on Poet's Corner, near Pembroke Lodge, within the northwest corner of the park. The solar-powered seat, erected in 2002, allows visitors to plug in and listen to eight of his songs as well as an interview.

The weight of history is palpable once you enter the former Royal Hunting Grounds through Richmond Gate, with 2,500 acres of unkempt and bucolic beauty stretched before you. Endless Henry VIIIs have been reimagined on these grounds, the most notable including Richard Burton in *Anne of the Thousand Days* (1969) and

Sid James in *Carry on Henry* (1971), who both wore the same costume. In fact, if you wanted to re-enact your own Henry and Anne (and have your hamper about you), you wouldn't be out of place, as Richmond Park has won the Warburtons annual Picnic Awards several years running.

The **Isabella Plantation** is a botanist's paradise. Every season sees a cornucopia of flora's finest, including camellias and magnolias in spring, azaleas and flowering rhododendrons from late April, dazzling displays of Japanese irises and day lilies in the summer, and guelder rose and berry-laden rowan and spindle trees in the autumn (and if the date is going downhill, just hand your partner a stinking hellebore as a subtle hint).

The park doesn't have to be explored on foot. For some live action, the **Kingston Riding Centre** offers hacks throughout the day, with specially curated Pimm's hacks and wine hunts. The safer (and equally romantic) option awaits non-horsey types over at Parkcycle, next to Roehampton Gate. But there is a third intrepid option, advisable only for the reckless dater: power kiting. **Kitevibe** swaps your horse for a kite and your buggy for a landboard on this most original of tours.

If heart rates need to be lowered, a walk or slow drive through the 1,600-strong herd of deer (red and fallow) grazing in the sunset is inescapably romantic. As the park closes at dusk, the smell of celebrated crêperie **Chez Lindsay**'s buckwheat crêpes – try the 'Super Complet' – draws hungry hordes to the bottom of Richmond Hill. End the day with a nightcap at one of the handful of pubs spilling out along the banks by Richmond Bridge. The real jewel in the crown, for both food and gardening, is the world-renowned **Petersham Nurseries** (see **Saved by the Hippies**, overleaf), near Terrace Gardens.

SAVED BY THE HIPPIES

Gael Boglione – a beautiful, bohemian Aussie ex-model who counts Richard E. Grant and Mick Jagger among her friends – and her husband Francesco, an Italian 'heepie' turned insurance broker, – are long-term residents of Petersham House, which the couple have transformed into one of the most prestigious homes in London. But these devoted owners endured a fierce battle with would-be developers over the adjoining nurseries. After a modest initial opening, the Bogliones received threatening letters from the council (all now posted on their website) for opening without a full restaurant licence.

Not only did the Bogliones prevent this little piece of Eden from being bulldozed, but they went on to collect furniture and artworks from all over the world to make it unique – tables from Italy with lead-covered tops, galvanized buckets from India, even an Antony Gormley sculpture which presides over the garden. The result is part modern colonial, part traditional English conservatory, and clearly reflects the couple's youth travelling in India and Morocco.

Their original chef, Skye Gyngell, had to build the kitchen up from scratch: what started with a four-burner stove and a grill so slow that it took two hours to cook an aubergine had developed into a Michelin-starred restaurant by 2011, with staff of twenty and all the ingredients she could hope for: for the Petersham chef the day begins with a forage in the Petersham gardens to find that produce ripe enough for the menu. After Gyngell's departure in 2012, another award-winning chef was appointed, Australian Greg Malouf.

FROM PORTRAITS TO PELICANS

. . . .

St James's Park

Much wine had passed, with grave
  discourse
Of who fucks who, and who does worse
(Such as you usually do hear
From those that diet at the Bear),
When I, who still take care to see
Drunkenness relieved by lechery,
Went out into St James's Park
To cool my head and fire my heart.

From 'A Ramble in St James's Park',
The Earl of Rochester

Back in the day of King James I, a menagerie of camels, crocodiles and elephants roamed the green 'plains' of **St James's Park**, only metres away from London's busy streets. The park has retained a little of its exotic heritage – the glassy lake teems with swans, great crested grebes, the odd flamingo and the five resident pelicans (see **From Russia With Love**, overleaf), best viewed from the Blue Bridge across the lake's centre. Looking east from the bridge, the government offices of Whitehall with their Kremlin-esque minarets, turrets and white façades, rise above the lake bordered by weeping willows. The meandering pathways that frame the lake are in stark contrast to the formal walkways around the park itself, which lead to some of London's most spectacular cultural and historical icons – the **National Gallery** and **National Portrait Gallery** to the east, the **Institute of Contemporary Arts** to the north, to the south a grand walk from Parliament Square to the Royal Mews, and **Buckingham Palace** to the west. With such a host of distractions, this royal park, the smallest of the seven, may easily be overlooked, but its charms are abundant and should not be missed.

Overlooking the lake, **Inn the Park** offers fried duck eggs and Welsh rarebit for brunch, and barbeques in the summer atop its curved wooden rooftop terrace. First thing in the morning, the lake is often shrouded by a thick cloak of fog, and at night, illuminated by the gaslights over the bridge (among the few remaining in London), the Headless Lady of the Lake has been seen to drift across the water. She was decapitated by her husband, the Sergeant of the Guards, in the 1780s, and he allegedly buried her head and dumped her body in the lake. After one sighting in 1804, two Coldstream Guards were committed to hospital with fright, and in 1972, a driver relied on the ghost story in court to successfully acquit himself of a dangerous driving charge after he had swerved to avoid her and crashed into a lamp post.

As the moon rises over Whitehall, and the pipistrelle bats emerge around the lake's edge, for a sundowner in summer the rooftop bar at the **Trafalgar Hotel** on Trafalgar Square has magical views of the capital, and in winter, the underground caverns of **Gordon's Wine Bar**, the oldest wine bar in London, are a cosy retreat from the cold. Candlelight illuminates the dank, dark brick arches of the interior, and 1940s posters adorn the walls to create an atmosphere that feels delightfully clandestine and seedy.

Caravaggio's depiction of the Last Supper, *Supper at Emmaus*, at the top of the central staircase of the **National Gallery**, sets the tone for dinner at the elegant rooftop restaurant at next door's **National Portrait Gallery**, overlooking Trafalgar Square and Westminster. As bedtime beckons, you'll find a sleeping David Beckham in the permanent collection in the gallery downstairs, a 2004 video installation piece by Sam Taylor-Wood.

The pelicans were first introduced into St James's Park by the Russian ambassador, who presented them to Charles II in 1664. In 1970 there was just one lone pelican, nicknamed 'the Lady of the Lake' (though she was actually called Daphne by the park keepers). Once again the Russians were approached to continue the tradition, and the ambassador obliged, presenting two pelicans from Astrakhan (named Astra and Khan). However, diplomatic relations were strained and anti-Soviet sentiment ignited when the two new arrivals started gobbling up the resident pigeons.

In 1995, after two Eastern European pelicans were donated to the Park, Lord Stoddart questioned in the House of Lords whether the conditions were conducive to mating, given that in 300 years there had not been a single pelican born. And so he asked, 'Is it kind to import those pelicans and so deny them a normal life with a mate, including the patter of tiny webbed feet?'

Today there are four pelicans among the exotic birds resident in St James's Park. Three were diplomatic gifts as their predecessors had been, but one just turned up out of the blue.

Pelicans' normal diet is fish, caught in their large bills, but in October 2006, one of the birds was the subject of a media furore after being photographed holding a pigeon in its beak for twenty minutes before swallowing it whole. You can watch them being fed (fish, not pigeons) near Duck Island Cottage between 2.30 and 3 pm daily, though one of them prefers to pinch fish for his lunch from the London Zoo.

 # SECRET GARDENS

St Dunstan in the East

St Dunstan's Hill, EC3

The bombed ruins of a medieval church and Wren tower whose walls and majestic windows have been decorated over time with Virginia creeper and an ornamental vine which turns crimson in the autumn, and has breathtaking blossoms in spring.

The Actors' Church

31 Bedford Street, WC2E 9ED

So called because of its historical ties with the theatre community surrounding it. The courtyard behind the Inigo Jones-designed St Paul's church feels undiscovered amid the bustle of Covent Garden, and is filled with roses and trees. It was here in 1662 that the first recorded performance of Punch and Judy (or Joan, as she was then known) took place.

The Quiet Garden in Memoriam of Basil Hume

Lamb's Passage, off Bunhill Row, EC1Y 8LE

An oasis for City workers in a former church car park. A tiny but incredibly lush space filled with jasmine bushes and bamboo.

St Mary's Secret Garden

50 Pearson Street, E2 8EL

A verdant Eden in the urban jungle that is Shoreditch comprising four interlinking areas: a natural woodland, a food-growing area, a herb and sensory garden and an area of herbaceous borders. The garden runs horticultural therapy for people with disabilities, but anyone can come here to find solace.

The Phoenix Garden

21 Stacey Street, WC2H 8DG

Home to the only frogs in the West End and it's easy to see why – a miniature meadow, echiums, red salvias, climbing clematis, brambles and a walnut tree which produces an abundant crop, collected by elderly Italians in the autumn.

Bonnington Square Garden

Kennington, SW8 1TQ

The pleasure garden here was once a bombsite and then a derelict playground before it was imaginatively redesigned by local residents. The garden includes an iron waterwheel, a huge Helping Hand sculpture, sub-tropical planting and a BYOB vegetarian café.

The Salters' Garden

. . . .

4 Fore Street, EC2Y 5DE

A mini-Versailles with rose bowers, urns, vistas and three fountains, flanked by the Roman city wall.

Postman's Park

. . . .

Little Britain, EC4M 7LS

Best known for the Watts Memorial, which commemorates Londoners who sacrificed their lives for others – lives which might otherwise have been forgotten. One of the most poignant inscriptions is for the eleven-year-old hero who cried, 'Mother, I saved him, but I could not save myself.'

Barnsbury Wood

. . . .

Crescent Street, N1 1BT

Even local residents have not heard of this delightful hidden woodland with wildlife garden which is also London's smallest Local Nature Reserve. Sadly it's only open on Tuesdays and (sometimes) Saturdays from 2 til 4 pm. Nearby are two contrasting gardens – 44 Hemingford Road is a lush country-style garden and 36 Thornhill Square's 120 foot-long garden has old roses, geraniums and clematis in curved beds.

Chelsea Physic Garden

. . . .

66 Royal Hospital Road, SW3 4HS

The garden itself is famous, but lesser known are its Snowdrop Days heralding the start of spring (and Valentine's Day). Discover dozens of different types of the *Galanthus* flowers on the Snowdrop Trail at a time of year when the garden is usually closed, and finish the tour with mulled wine at the Tangerine Dream Café.

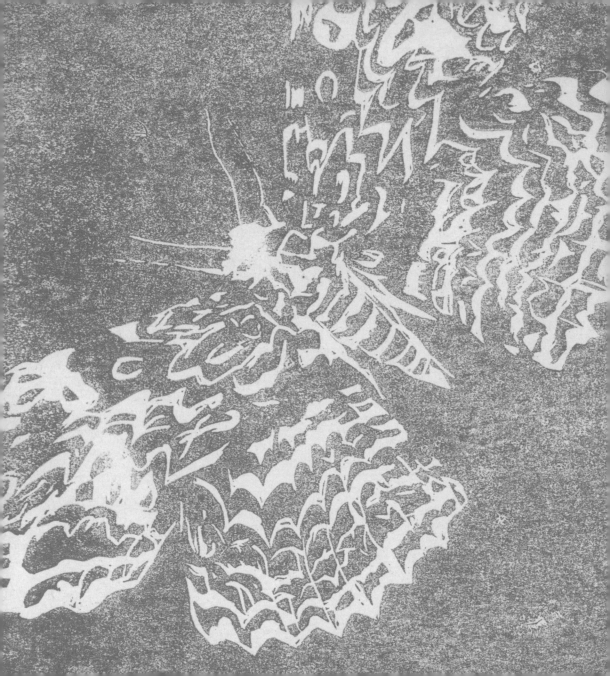

FROM KINGSLAND ROAD TO RIDLEY ROAD

. . . .

Dalston

The sheer diversity of people and businesses that Dalston now prides itself on feels a long way from its rural beginnings – the neighbourhood's name was derived from Deorlaf's tun or farm. A more tangible connection with Dalston's past is in its music venues; it has always been legendary as a hub of entertainment centres – for example, the Dalston Theatre, formerly a hippodrome and music hall built to house Robert Fossett's Circus, which became the Four Aces Blues Club, London's best-known reggae venue and scene of many fierce 'soundclashes' in the 1970s.

With a long night in store, it makes sense to kick off with **A Little of What You Fancy**, and in the case of this atmospheric restaurant, that's actually quite a lot of excellent British fare, with a subtle touch of French.

The clipboard menus, wooden boxes of lemons and oranges dotted about the place, tables salvaged from a school and little details like a sign that reads 'Eggs for Sale' underneath a T-shirt inscribed with the word 'Chips' set a decidedly homely atmosphere.

Short and sweet Ashwin Street manages to pack in a fair few of Dalston's go-to spots. The **Arcola Theatre** is no longer resident to its namesake street, having upsized to Ashwin Street while maintaining the industrial aesthetic which has been the backdrop to so many of its diverse (often politically charged) plays over the years. Next door, **Café Oto** was named by Italian *Vogue* as Britain's coolest venue and, with a name that means both 'noise' and 'music' in Japanese, it might easily be mistaken for yet another hipster

joint too loud and self-important to hear yourself think. However, it is in fact a distinctly no-frills joint which set out to champion underground music and has stuck to its guns. They don't do mainstream, although when Sean Lennon did a gig there, his mother, Yoko Ono, got up to perform a couple of tracks with him. At the Print House next door, membership cards are dispensed to all and sundry (for notifications of concerts and events rather than exclusivity) by the enthusiastic doorman for the **Dalston Roof Park**, up four flights of steps and out onto a grass-decked roof garden. Couples and small groups are strewn across deckchairs and wooden garden furniture, cradling frozen margaritas and souvlaki from the BBQ. It's worth bringing a blanket to share as the night wears on.

The atmosphere at the **Dalston Jazz Bar** depends on what time you wind up there; earlier in the evening there are bookshelves to borrow from, a soundtrack of soul, even free cheese and biscuits. Later on and into the early hours the fishbowl windows steam up as the tiny space becomes crammed – note: this is no place for genuine jazz lovers. The nearby **Vortex Jazz Club** is a better bet for

the 'no-talking' ethos of real jazz aficionados.

Late-night kebabs might not feel like the right vibe on a couple's tour of Dalston, but this is the capital of London's Turkish community and the area's social clubs, hot nut shops, ocakbasi (charcoal grill) restaurants and iskender kebab houses, and **Mangal** in Arcola Street is the jewel in the crown and is unmissable. It's BYOB if you're eating in and while the billowing smoke and seeming chaos of the open kitchen-cum-foyer might seem impenetrable at first, it's well worth pushing through to the tables tucked away at the back. Keeping it in the family, the **Efes Pool Club and Bar** happily does what it says on the door. It's unpretentious and the dozens of pool tables are by no means reserved for regulars – the usual 'quid on table' rules apply. It's open til 4 am, so caters to the pre- and after-party pool player.

One of the bars that has the area's entrepreneurial and community spirit written all over it is **Ridley Road Market Bar**, which has given the area on the street out front to an array of stall-owners, open until midnight and very good for late-night munchies, from Big Apple Hot Dogs to Luca's Italian meatball sandwiches. Back in 1947, known then by the Fascists as Yiddley Road, Ridley Road Market was the scene of the biggest and most regular 'clashes' between the Jewish 43 Group and the post-war Fascists (see **Not Just a Hairdresser**, opposite). And as the Market Bar closes, the beautiful art deco **Rio Cinema** up the road remains one of London's only champions of the midnight movie screening.

The later it gets, the harder it becomes to ignore the distant pulse of myriad dancefloors, calling from the depths of one basement bar after another. For the full package, **Dalston Superstore**

does Berlin-style, laid-back café upstairs, dirty bass lines on a fulsome sound system downstairs. It's officially a 'gay' bar but a long way from G.A.Y. The slightly more refined option is **The Alibi**, down the inevitable steep set of unmarked stairs that lead to an unpretentious warren of exposed brickwork, wooden booths and cosy dancefloors. Finally, if you're in the mood to throw yourself into some proper clubbing without setting out for one of the big names, within spitting distance the **The Nest**, as its name suggests, boasts a series of intimate booths, and plays house and electro all night long.

NOT JUST A HAIRDRESSER

Even after World War II, when the world had been shown the scale of the Holocaust, Oswald Mosley's blackshirts still had plenty of support in the East End, as he sought to stir hatred against the large Jewish communities there. A very young Vidal Sassoon was part of the 43 Group – so named because of the number of ex-servicemen who turned up to the first meeting – who were disgusted by the Attlee government's failure to ban fascism in the UK and determined to take the law into their own hands and thwart Mosley's men.

Dalston proved the epicentre of much of the combat; the group wore cricket boxes to protect themselves from being kneed in the crotch by the huge numbers of policemen enlisted to 'keep order'. The Dalston synagogue was smashed and the Nazi Horst Wessel Song was sung after pubs closed; consequently the 43 Group struck back, ensuring that they closed down any Fascist meetings before they could start, as it was the incitement of attacks against them that proved the most dangerous.

On one occasion, Sassoon returned to work after a skirmish, sporting a black eye. When asked about it, he told his employer that he'd tripped over a hairpin.

FROM EXMOUTH MARKET
TO LUCKY VOICE

. . . .

Islington

Once one of the seedier and more run-down areas of central London, **Exmouth Market** is now pedestrianised, vibrant, and teeming with independent bars, boutiques, restaurants and galleries. On a summer's evening, sitting out in the street underneath patio heaters, munching tapas and drinking Rioja, you could almost imagine you are in a little village in Spain.

It's a nice stretch to do a mini bar crawl: kick-start your evening downstairs at **Dollar Bar and Grill** with its pornstar martinis (passion fruit, vanilla and vodka with a champagne chaser) then move on to a match or two of babyfoot at **Café Kick**, where the football tables are squeezed between the bar counter (decorated with bright bottle labels) and the terrace. True to its Spanish roots,

on offer are exotic beers, from Estrella Damm to Super Bock and Nastro Azzurro, and small plates of tasty snacks. For more substantial tapas, **Morito** or **Caravan** are equally inviting.

Less well-known perhaps to the local media types who line the streets each evening is that Exmouth Market is home to one of the world's most respected tattoo artists, Mo Coppoletta, whose studio **The Family Business** is filled with all manner of objets, religious iconography and portfolios – the studio was launched with the intent to bring a fresh approach to the art form with each tattoo created from a bespoke design. Mo's premise is to create tasteful tattoos for first-timers, old-timers and serious collectors – lovers with an impulse for his and hers may or may not take inspiration from a

Damien Hirst-designed tattoo (see **Body Art**, p50).

Round the corner, on Rosebery Avenue, lies one of London's leading dance venues, **Sadler's Wells**. Attracting the world's best contemporary troupes from Rambert to Nederlands Dance Company, this sixth iteration of the building since it first opened in 1683 is strikingly modern in sleek steel and glass, and since the great Lilian Baylis took charge in the 1920s, it has welcomed the world's greatest dancers. From Matthew Bourne's *Edward Scissorhands* to ZooNation's *Some Like It Hip Hop* or Tanztheater Wuppertal Pina Bausch on tour, the programme genuinely ranges from the mainstream to the cutting-edge.

At the top of Rosebery Avenue is The Angel Islington. It was named after The Angel Inn, a local landmark in Jacobean times, during which the area was known as Merry Islington for its varied entertainment centres. Back then, the Collins Music Hall, the Grand Theatre and the Philharmonic Hall were all situated there and, being outside London, Angel became a refuge after the plagues and the Great Fire. The Angel Inn is now a bank, but the main drag of Upper Street continues the legacy of merriment as the most densely bar- and restaurant-populated street in London. But the best spots are to be found off the beaten track. **The Charles Lamb** is delightfully atmospheric, with its weathered Victorian tiles, tree stump doorstops and higgledy-piggledy furniture. Its

French culinary influences as well as an annual Bastille Day boules tournament betray owner Camille Hobby-Limon's nationality. Hobby-Limon also co-created the nearby **69 Colebrooke Row**, the 'bar with no name', which has taxidermy and old paintings on the walls. In keeping with its 1920 speakeasy style, all of the staff are dressed in vintage outfits. Head mixologist Tony Conigliaro is widely known as one of the UK's pioneering drinks creators and even gives cocktail masterclasses, where you can learn how to mix the classics.

A stroll down **Camden Passage**, which by day is one of London's best antique markets with everything from beaded 1940s purses to coins from the Russian revolution, takes you past the superbly named **The Elk in the Woods**, an inner-city take on a stylish countryside hunters' pub, with rough oak tables and antlers and skulls mounted on the wooden walls.

Further along Upper Street are the **Almeida Theatre** and the **King's Head Theatre**, both favourites with locals and those from further afield. The former attracts the bigger names, with Gemma Arterton, Carey Mulligan and Jonathan Pryce treading its boards in recent times. It puts on new work and classics, as well as an annual summer festival of contemporary opera, music and theatre. Its neighbour, the King's Head, is one of the London fringe's leading lights and manages to cram an impressive quota of opera, musicals and plays into its limited, pew-strewn space.

Less high-brow but equally entertaining is Martha Lane Fox's **Lucky Voice**, at the classy end of the karaoke spectrum. This is no public scrum of embarrassment in front of strangers; this is a swanky bar connected to a warren of intimate private booths. There's even a playlist named 'songs for non-singers' and a THIRSTY button that summons a drinks waitress when pressed.

A final stop, which has deep leather sofas to sink into, is **Public House**, with low lighting and drippy candles wedged into wine bottles (ideal date territory). The house speciality is champagne, home-made vanilla bitters and fig liqueur served over a sugar cube rubbed with lemon zest. Monday offers taste testing and Tuesday has a live pianist, but perhaps the *coup de théâtre* is the Latin harpist on a Wednesday.

BODY ART

In 2011, Roman Abramovitch's girlfriend Dasha Zhukova launched a new magazine, *Garage*, aimed at bringing together individuals from diverse creative fields to produce something compelling and bold. Her first project, INKED, did exactly that, calling on some of the world's most lauded living artists – Jeff Koons, the Chapman Brothers, Richard Prince – to create tattoos for the magazine which would then be emblazoned onto willing human canvasses – real people who were up for it, as opposed to models or tattoo specialists.

The tattoo to hit the headlines and make the cover of the magazine was designed by Damien Hirst, tattooed by Mo Coppoletta, and the woman in question was twenty-three-year-old Shauna Taylor. The tattoo was a pair of butterfly wings which appeared on Taylor's labia majora and mons pubis, her pudendal cleft forming the insect's thorax and abdomen. The magazine cover went on sale with a green butterfly-shaped modesty sticker covering Taylor's crotch with a note reading 'peel slowly and see', but certain shops, including WHSmith in the UK, refused to stock it.

When asked why she agreed to it, Taylor answered with the perhaps dubious accolade, 'Not one single person can ever say they gave birth through a Damien Hirst piece of art.'

FROM GREAT WINDMILL STREET TO DEAN STREET

. . . .

The Seven Noses of Soho

In 1997, people started to notice plaster noses fixed to public buildings around London. Inevitably a number of urban myths sprang up. A favourite of taxi drivers was that he who found all 'seven noses of Soho' would win infinite wealth. Last October an artist from Hackney, Rick Buckley, outed himself as the man behind the noses (see **Blown it!**, p57). A stone's throw from each of these noses are some of central London's most inviting and original late-night venues, waiting to be sniffed out. As night falls on the abundance of intoxicating bars, seedy window displays and trendy cafés that make up the area, the choice can seem overwhelming to the uninitiated. But let the seven noses be your guide on this after-dark tour of Soho …

Being jam-packed with strip bars, including the infamous Windmill Club itself, Great Windmill Street is a good place to start off the evening, before its red lights are turned on. For an early evening cocktail, the latest offering from chef and restaurateur Mark Hix, the subterranean **Mark's Bar**, is just around the corner from nose number one. With battered antique furniture scattered about the space, moodily lit by vintage lamps, the bar has a sexy, timeless atmosphere. The cocktails range from the classic to the retro: the Hanky Panky combines Beefeater gin, Fernet Branca and vermouth. But you can also order a gleaming tankard full of one of Hix's various pale ales, bitters, stouts and even own-brand porter.

A walk down Shaftesbury Avenue in search of the next nose takes in theatreland's glittering billboards with the **Criterion Theatre**, on Piccadilly Circus. The theatre, one of the West End's most beautiful and intimate, is completely underground, a fact that the BBC made use of during WWII, shifting its headquarters there as a safe haven during the Blitz. Down Haymarket to **Admiralty Arch**, the stunning tri-arched gateway from the Mall to Trafalgar Square, is home to the second nose, on the inside wall of the northernmost arch. The nose is at a height of about seven feet and sits at head height for anyone riding through the arch on a horse, giving weight to the urban myth that it belongs to Wellington (famed for his particularly large hooter) and is rubbed by cavalry for luck as they pass through the arch. An even more tenuous myth was that it is a spare for the statue of Nelson who stands atop his column in the nearby square. Three cultural giants in the vicinity, the **National Gallery**, the **National Portrait Gallery** and the **ICA** stay open until 9 pm on Thursdays and Fridays, with talks, tours, workshops, salons and even drop-in drawing sessions as part of their late-night offerings.

Up St Martin's Lane, past Leicester Square's brand new restaurant, casino and music venue, **Heliot** (on the site of the former Hippodrome), where the drinks are designed by celebrated mixologist Tony Conigliaro (see p49) and which is open until 5 am, Floral Street has the handiwork of a rival artist, where not a nose but an ear protrudes from one of the walls. Nearby Endell Street is the next destination on the great nasal hunt, as well as this walk's dinner pit stop. **Circus** is not everyone's cup of tea – some have dubbed it a gimmick, others a quirky night of fun. As the name suggests, dinner – pan-American cuisine – is served among a plethora of cabaret acts, from contortionist acrobats to flame-swallowing dancers. You can choose to sit at a long wooden table – the 'stage table' – which doubles as a performance runway. Circus's interior design is one of its most talked about features – the work of the iconic Tom Dixon – from the surrealist foyer, a world of smoke and mirrors, to the futuristic black, white and silver of the main space. For those who prefer not to mix food with hoop-based balancing acts, **Da Mario** does traditional and intimate Italian, the kind of place where waiters and customers are on first-name terms – a rare thing in central London.

Seeking out the remaining noses late at night may become challenging, but back in Soho proper, D'Arblay Street has nose number four, and tapas hotspot **Copita**, which means 'sherry glass', making it the perfect spot for a sweet Pedro Ximenez served in the tall thin namesake glass, perhaps accompanied by a crispy custard tart. The next nose is on the outside of **Milk Bar**, on Bateman Street – closed at this hour, but during the daytime serving the best flat whites in London, and a favourite with local entrepreneurs and media types. The legendary jazz club **Ronnie Scott's** is round the corner on Frith Street, and opens its doors for its late weeknight performances, The Late Late Show, where punters are even invited to jam as long as they happen to have brought along their instrument of choice. Cocktail in hand, tapping your foot along to the syncopated beats, this feels like a suitably refined and sexy end to the evening. But if you have the energy to seek out the remaining noses, the next is at nearby Meard Street, a favourite with French tourists for its pun on the French for 'shit' (merde). At no. 7 Meard Street you'll find a sign outside declaring 'This is not a brothel. There are no prostitutes at this address'. Apparently this was an in-joke from the late dandy artist Sebastian Horsley who lived there (and it did used to be a brothel). The final nose is on the neighbouring Dean Street. More recently, **Soho Theatre** has become the go-to destination for all the latest comedians hailing from the Edinburgh and Melbourne festivals. But if exhaustion is setting in, on the corner of Meard and Dean, you can rest your weary heads at the **Dean Street Townhouse**, part of the acclaimed Soho House group but open to the general public. With the smallest rooms practically the price of a Travelodge, and with its classic, transatlantic chic, the Townhouse hotel is the perfect end to a Soho sojourn. Some of the bedroom windows even offer a ringside view of the Groucho Club entrance – the ideal position to spot a drunken celebrity or two.

BLOWN IT!

Artist Rick Buckley, the man behind the noses, revealed that they had been a protest at the rise of the all-consuming 'Big Brother' society, and were modelled on his own nose. At the time when the debate was fiercest over infringement of liberty, with CCTV cameras at every street corner, Buckley became inspired by the situationists, artists and writers who protested through sporadic illegal actions – a form of performance art. At the time, Buckley fixed thirty-five noses to various walls all over London, but the seven of Soho are among the few that remain.

FROM FIRST THURSDAY
TO LAST ORDERS

. . . .

Shoreditch

Over the past few years, Shoreditch has earned its place as London's cultural and social heart – where nights grow longer and later with fashion, art, music, food and dancing on tap. The epitome of its forward-thinking spirit is **First Thursdays**, which keeps 134 different east London galleries open until 9 pm on the first Thursday of each month. Those who do it by the book can start at Whitechapel Gallery and follow a guided tour to a selection of galleries, where curators, writers, academics and artists share their knowledge and passion. Alternatively, the more intrepid can download a map at www.firstthursdays.co.uk and carve their own spontaneous path. But this is no tour of the old masters or impressionists; much of the art revels in just how contemporary it is. The Vyner Street area around Bethnal Green is the most experimental and is best for window-shopping, or on occasion, perplexed gawping; for buyers, the commercial galleries are scattered around Old Street. The art is not only in the confines of gallery spaces; there's barely a disused wall, archway or underpass without the handiwork of one of Shoreditch's famous street artists, from the best of the US, Shepherd Fairey, to the controversial Banksy, whose tagging war with graffiti king Robbo has dominated the scene (see **Banksy v. Robbo**, p64) for the past few years.

Depending on which night you pop in, **Ninetyeight Bar and Lounge**, on Curtain Road, might be serving up jazz, DJ nights or sonnet readings, and the cocktails to accompany the live performances are just as theatrical, with everything from lavender blended with gin to spearmints in Sambuca: 'If

it's crazy, we do it', the owner has claimed. And given the bar features home-made candles with lickable flavoured wax, it's hard to argue with that. There's a piano outside for some streetside dueting and a toy train that carries shot glasses full of baked-beaned Bloody Marys and sugar cubes up and down the gilt-edged bar. Another local option for an eccentric aperitif is **Callooh Callay**, named after Lewis Carroll's nonsensical 'Jabberwocky' poem, where cocktails are served from gramophones, and in homage to yet another Lewis (C. S.), entry to the rear lounge and to the cassette-tape-covered loo is through a Narnia-style wardrobe.

When it comes to cuisine, Shoreditch has offerings from almost every country, but in particular from Vietnam. The best is **Cay Tre**,

unassuming from the outside yet with a telling queue curling out the door, but they'll serve you a bottle of wine while you wait for summer rolls and hot bowls of pho. For honest British food underneath the neon lights of Tracy Emin's *Life Without You Never*, the **Rivington Bar and Grill** attracts arty types and even has a Leader Board, which rates local galleries and shows. Equally crammed with hipsters in the lovely Tea Building is **Pizza East**, which has huge but surprisingly intimate wooden tables and industrial décor, as does the bar it sits on top of, **Concrete**, an underground venue with storytelling nights, literary death matches and musical bingo.

Nearby, **The Book Club** has a great sense of humour about the area and some of its inhabitants with its self-referential cocktails such

as Shoreditch Twat and Don't Go to Dalston. Thanks to the sheer imagination of their events, ranging from Come and Get Felt Up (a nostalgic craft night involving pipecleaners, glue and felt) or Tweetbox, a night where you can tweet your musical requests in advance, this has really become one of the creative hubs of Shoreditch. Another contender for that title is **Shoreditch Town Hall**, which has recently reopened and when it has finished its refurbishment, will be bigger than the Battersea Arts Centre and feature some of the country's most exciting emerging theatre and opera companies.

A short walk away from the bustling epicentre lies a haven of exquisite curated culture as well as a modern design masterpiece, **Rich Mix**. En route to one of the three cinema screens which play both mainstream and indie flicks, audiences must weave through a mezzanine gallery overlooking the main stage, from which art shows, musical performances or even the epic Pongathon (a table tennis party) can be glimpsed. In the summer months, the nearby **Queen of Hoxton** hosts a rooftop cinema.

The appropriately named **Nightjar** is the place to go for a nightcap, and only caters to those 'in the know', with no sign on the door except a brass plate with a nightjar on it. It's worth making a booking as this is seating only, but it's a trip back in time worth making. The bar is arranged as a 1930s scene, with candlelit tables, cocktails organised into pre-prohibition, prohibition, post-war and signature, and live swing or jazz bands as the soundtrack.

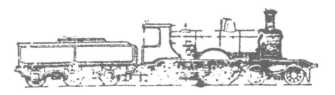

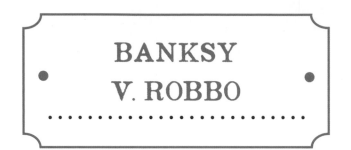

BANKSY V. ROBBO

For years, many have worshipped at the altar of street artist Banksy, with local councils even deeming to place Perspex sheets over certain works to protect them from being vandalised – a strange paradox given the long-term battle between graffiti specialists and the owners of the walls they decorate.

However, in late 2009, Banksy committed the ultimate graf faux pas – he painted over a legendary piece of veteran graffitist Robbo's work that had remained untouched for nearly twenty-five years on Camden Canal. The work, painted in 1985, was one of London's earliest pieces of street art. Banksy added a stencil of a workman plastering over Robbo's work as a commentary that Robbo was 'past it'. Robbo promptly came out of retirement, donned a wetsuit, crossed the canal on a blow-up lilo and retaliated by manipulating Banksy's workman to make it look like he was painting the words 'King Robbo' as a tribute. Banksy, after much deliberation, then added the prefix 'FUC' to 'King Robbo', and Robbo has been defacing Banksy's pieces ever since.

The underlying debate behind the public spat is about street art versus graffiti. While, thanks to Banksy, the scene has become better understood and even protected, there remains an uneasiness among his peers about the commercialism of his work. Some argue that to label something as street art puts financial value on it and that the mass production of Banksy's stencillings is created with the wrong intentions.

PLACES TO LAY YOUR HEAD

A selection of London's most unique hotels for you
to rest your weary heads after a late night out …

The Zetter Townhouse

49–50 St John's Square, EC1V 4JJ

Upstairs, each room is unique,
designed with rich colours and
mahogany four-poster beds. Almost
all whims will be satisfied by its
Michelin-starred restaurant, a
games room with ping-pong and
Nintendo Wii and a fine cocktail bar.

Charlotte Street Hotel

15–17 Charlotte Street, W1T 1RJ

A stylish hotel on one of the most
charming streets in London. Fifty-two
rooms in a modern English style, with
high windows that let the light pour in
and views stretching over the rooftops
of Soho and Covent Garden.

Number Sixteen

• • • • • • • • • • • • • • • • • • • •

16 Sumner Place, SW7 3EG

Furnished with grace and taste and filled with objects of beauty: collages of butterflies, driftwood furniture, a Victorian birdcage. Sitting in its beautiful tree-lined garden you could almost be in the south of France.

Hazlitt's

• • • • • • • • • • • • • • • • • • • •

6 Frith Street, W1D 3JA

A captivating boutique hotel hidden in Soho with authentic eighteenth-century furnishings. Frith Street was a fashionable address for the literati of the time, and all of Hazlitt's rooms are named after distinguished residents and visitors to the houses.

York & Albany

• • • • • • • • • • • • • • • • • • • •

127–129 Parkway, NW1 7PS

Gordon Ramsay's celebrated restaurant has an equally elegant hotel attached to it. With just nine rooms, be sure to ask for one with a view over Regent's Park.

40 Winks

• • • • • • • • • • • • • • • • • • • •

109 Mile End Road, E1 4UJ

This eccentric 'micro-boutique hotel' has a 'home away from home' ethos – all thanks to its owner's commitment to his guests. If you are too late to book, the hotel opens its doors to a wider audience with intriguing soirées such as Bedtime Stories, for which guests are encouraged to wear their pajamas.

Claridge's

Brook Street, W1K 4HR

The most iconic luxury hotel in London. Famous for its afternoon tea and celebrity guests – its close association with the Royal family has even led to it being referred to as 'an extension to Buckingham Palace'.

CitizenM Bankside

20 Lavington Street, SE1 0NZ

Located close to the Tate Modern, the aim of this international chain, which has recently opened its doors in London, is 'to create affordable luxury for the people ... The explorers, adventurers and dreamers. Those who travel the world with big hearts and wide eyes.' And thankfully, those with small wallets too.

Rough Luxe

1 Birkenhead Street, WC1H 8BA

A little bit of luxury in a rough – albeit rapidly gentrifying – part of London. Bare floorboards and old chipped paintwork are offset with statement bathtubs and contemporary art. Owner Leo and his dog Spud (who has his own website at myspud.co.uk) will make you feel like guests in their home.

The Rookery Hotel

Cowcross Street, London EC1M 6DS

A Georgian-styled boutique hotel a stone's throw from the architectural delights of Smithfield Market and The City, and foodie destinations St John and Hix. Don't miss the extraordinary top floor Rook's Nest suite with its 40 foot octagonal spire and views over St Paul's and the Old Bailey.

FROM BUENOS AIRES
TO EAST INDIA

. . . .

Greenwich

The **Docklands Light Railway** might just be London's closest equivalent to a Venetian gondola, for this tour freewheels through some of London's oldest man-made wonders. The 'premium' seats are right up at the front of this driverless train, with rollercoaster views of everything from the Olympic Park to locals' front rooms.

A short walk from Greenwich station, this east-end adventure starts with Argentina's favourite hot drink, a *submarino* (bar of dark chocolate dunked in a glass of hot milk) accompanied by all the Saturday papers in the **Buenos Aires Café** on Royal Hill. From the ocean deep to the stratosphere, Greenwich Park offers star-crossed lovers Christopher Wren's stunning **Royal Observatory**, a brisk climb from the Circus Gate entrance

to the top of Constitution Hill. As well as spectacular views over London, the observatory hosts the world-famous Prime Meridian, Longitude 0°, where you can stand with one foot in the west and one foot in the east. There's no longer water in it, but Princess Caroline's famous sunken bath at the southern end of the park tells a story of defiance and mischief (see **Royal Bathtime**, p75).

Leaving the park at Park Row gate, pass the National Maritime Museum to the **Old Royal Naval College**, home to a host of buildings designed by Wren and his assistant Hawksmoor, most famously The Painted Hall – considered the finest dining hall in the western world – an apt location for Angelina Jolie's 'Illuminati gathering' scene in the first *Tomb Raider* movie. In the Lower Hall, enthroned in

Heaven with the Virtues behind them, are depicted one of history's best-known ruling couples, William and Mary of Orange.

If Thornhill's masterpiece (which took nineteen years to complete) has inspired a sudden wave of creativity, the nearby **Biscuit Ceramic Café** invites visitors to choose ceramic items – from teapots to vases – and decorate them with their own designs. Items are then fired in the café's kiln and can be delivered to your home. At the entrance to the nearby **Greenwich Market**, the BananaMan stall offers passers-by fruit dipped in Belgian chocolate on weekends.

An innocuous pathway along the side of the famous *Cutty Sark* tea clipper leads to a glass dome, the entrance to the **Greenwich foot tunnel**, where cyclists are supposed to dismount but can't resist the never-ending, neon-lit tunnel reminiscent of a science-fiction time portal. Time stands still at the other end at **Island Gardens Park**, where the view across the river of the Royal Naval College buildings is exactly what Canaletto himself saw back in the eighteenth century.

Board the DLR at Island Gardens, and one stop later, at Mudchute, Canary Wharf skyscrapers rise up above the Anglo-Nubian goats (half goat, half

rabbit, it would apear) of Europe's largest city farm, the **Mudchute Park and Farm**. Rumour has it that critter-stroking can bring out maternal instincts, so perhaps baby llamas, cows and sheep should be treated with caution.

Two stops above Mudchute on the DLR, alight at South Quay for **The Gun**, a beautiful early-nineteenth-century listed public house, now gastropub, offering locally sourced seafood and an array of roast dinners on Sunday. If you haven't booked, there are tables by the fire at the back, and on the river terrace. The River Room upstairs was the preferred rendezvous location for Lord Nelson and his mistress

Lady Emma Hamilton. Her husband tolerated the affair out of respect for Nelson and in time the three ended up living together openly, in a celebrity ménage à trois that fascinated the adoring public. The pub was also a landing point for smugglers unloading contraband on the site and distributing it via a hidden tunnel. There is still a spy-hole in the secret circular staircase to watch out for 'The Revenue Men'.

Alternatively, **Fatboy's Diner** (a 'bear with me' detour via East India DLR), will transport you straight back to the 1950s, with its 'Burn it and Let it Swim' (chocolate ice cream afloat in coke) and 'New York Hound' (steamed hot dog with sauerkraut).

ROYAL BATHTIME

When George IV married Princess Caroline of Brunswick, it was not willingly – the extravagant prince was heavily in debt and the only solution was to marry and produce an heir, so that the government would pay off his debts. That he found her unattractive and unhygienic was unfortunately part of the bargain. As soon as he set eyes on her, he declared himself sick and called for a stiff drink.

Their sex life was brief and unspectacular. He didn't mince his words: 'It required no small [effort] to conquer my aversion and overcome the disgust of her person.' She, on the other hand, claimed he was 'fat and nothing like as handsome as his portrait' and so drunk that he spent the better part of the night 'under the grate, where he fell, and where I left him'.

However, the licentious Princess Caroline was unfazed, holding lavish parties and soirées, where all manner of debauchery took place. Perhaps in a nod to her husband's complaints of 'malodorousness', she had a giant tiled plunge bath made, and invited admirals, captains and politicians to join her in it. She even went to trial for adultery with a low-born man, during which she joked that she had indeed committed adultery once – with the husband of Mrs Fitzherbert, the King's long-term mistress.

When she finally left England to live abroad, the King ordered that her home, Montague House, be razed to the ground. It is a suitable irony that a woman who was castigated for being 'unclean' all her life lives on in the heart of Greenwich through the surviving remains of her sunken bath.

FROM HUNGERFORD BRIDGE TO OXO TOWER

. . . .

The South Bank

The South Bank, dominated by the iconic **National Theatre**, **Royal Festival Hall** and **London Eye**, clearly has plenty to offer the conscientious planner. But less known is its ability to deliver an equally diverse and diverting trail for the more spontaneous of lovers.

The pedestrian-only Hungerford Bridge is easily the most atmospheric Thames crossing with its suspension stays fanning out like peacock feathers on either side. A prearranged rendezvous at the Embankment end is the perfect excuse for crossing the river, while looking northbound Waterloo Bridge is the scene of Hugh Grant's declaration of love for co-star Andie MacDowell in the hit film *Four Weddings and a Funeral*.

Unavoidable (with its 21 acres of real estate) is the **Southbank Centre**,

Europe's largest centre for the arts, with lots to offer last-minute merchants: for the more bookish duo, the **Saison Poetry Library** is a good place to hunt for your favourite poet from the most comprehensive and accessible collection of modern poetry in all of Britain.

An eastbound stroll along the riverbank is a visual feast. The graffiti-laced nooks and crannies are home to London's most committed skateboarders, and on a good day, even the freerunners and capoeiristas provide breathtaking free entertainment. Tucked underneath Waterloo Bridge is possibly the most romantic spot of the lot – the **Southbank book market**. Row upon row of trestle tables covered with dusty old books line the pavement, inviting the passer-by

to rediscover childhood friends or forgotten love stories.

Every summer the concrete pavement in front of the National Theatre is transformed into Theatre Square, with its fake lawns, giant topiary chair (which makes a good perch for two) and optimistically placed deckchairs, bustling with theatre, fire, circus, juggling, music dance and street performance, all part of the Watch This Space festival. If you're feeling confident, there are 'taster' sessions of swing dancing or even acrobatics. For the less co-ordinated, simply sit and soak it up from one of the many wooden benches lining the Upper Ground bank, one of which (if you can find it), hosts a plaintive ode to riverside loneliness: 'Memorial to the Unknown Husband. Often Imagined. Much Desired. Never Found.'

Further along the riverbank the colourful Ampersand sculpture, in the courtyard of the Oxo Tower, begs a cheesy self-timed photo on either side. The **Oxo Tower**'s famous restaurant and brasserie may be fully booked, but more original is a trip straight to the fifth floor to stand outside on the balcony to admire the lights of London over a 'Summer of Love' cocktail for which the bar manager recently won the No. 209 Gin Duel (see **Summer of Love**, overleaf).

Leaving the river, head down to the Cut, and foodie destination pub the **Anchor & Hope**, with an ethos of 'no bookings, shared tables, down to earth, always busy'. It's worth the wait.

SUMMER OF LOVE

In April 2011, the annual international cocktail competition was held in San Francisco. One of the finalists, Ian Goodman, the bartender from London's Oxo Tower, was pitting his Summer of Love against another Londoner, Alessandro Paludet of 22 Below. Each competitor had 209 seconds to make and serve their winning aperitif-style cocktail, in a competition that started at 2:09. The winner was the Summer of Love. The finalists' cocktails all used No. 209 Gin as a base but the rest was for them to decide. Goodman's and Paludet's recipes were as follows:

Summer of Love

A generous shot of 209 gin dashed with elderflower, peach and ginger liqueurs. Shaken with orange flower water and fresh lemon mix. Absinthe rinse. Served straight up.

Inspired by San Francisco's place in history as a centre of 1960s counterculture and Scott McKenzie's classic anthem, the flavours combine to be zingy, light, fragrant and refreshing. Perfect for summer quaffing.

Ingredients
50ml 209 gin
15ml crème de pèche
15ml St-Germain elderflower liqueur
15ml Domaine de Canton ginger liqueur
50ml lemon juice
½ to 1 fresh egg white

*5 drops Bitter Truth Orange Flower
  Water*
La Fée Absinthe rinse

Method
- Coat the inside of a 200ml pony/
  sours glass with absinthe and discard
  any liquid.
- Vigorously shake remaining
  ingredients over cubed ice. Strain
  into glass.
- Garnish with lemon twist and borage
  blossom.

Pool of London Fizz

A large slug of 209 gin, raspberry
ripple and Earl Grey cordial, shaken
with Repeal Bitters and fresh lemon
mix. Built over cubed ice. Club soda
charge.

This cocktail amplifies the bergamot
present in the gin married with
syrup of fresh raspberry, vanilla and
citrus peel. An added hint of spicy
complexity of the bitters brings
together the profile of the gin and
Earl Grey. The name is associated
with the Oxo Tower's location
overlooking the River Thames in the
centre of London.

Ingredients
50ml 209 gin
15ml raspberry ripple syrup
20ml fresh Earl Grey tea cordial
50ml lemon juice
½ to 1 fresh egg white
5 drops Bitter Truth Repeal Bitters
Soda/seltzer charge

Method
- Combine all ingredients except the
  soda water, hard shake over cubed ice.
- Double strain into collins or highball
  glass over fresh cubed ice.
- Charge with the soda water and
  garnish with orange twist and fresh
  raspberry.

FROM MALTBY STREET TO SOUTHWARK CATHEDRAL

Bermondsey

Oh God! People having no water to drink but the water of the common sewer which stagnates full of dead fish, cats and dogs.

Charles Kingsley, on Bermondsey

Contrary to Kingsley's claims, Bermondsey is now the place to be. **Borough Market** draws crowds from all over London but real locals hit nearby Druid Street and Maltby Street, starting at **St John Bakery** for the most delicious custard- and fruit-filled doughnuts and Eccles cakes in all of London. Visit Monmouth Coffee for a morning espresso before wandering the bricked archway warehouses around Lassco for quality antiques. Maltby Street market spreads itself generously over a number of streets and, every Saturday morning, storage units hoist their shutters to reveal cheese, fresh fruit and veg, organic meat, and more.

However, Borough Market is obviously the original and shouldn't be overlooked, not least because of the dizzying choice of aphrodisiac – savoury chocolate dishes from Rabot Estate, oysters from Wright Brothers or asparagus from the amiable John Stark (better known as Jock). Bermondsey Square is also home to the weekly Antiques Market, every Friday, come rain or shine – once known as the only place that thieves could sell stolen goods with impunity. Ping-pong tables are scattered invitingly among the stalls for the more competitive couple.

The green outside **Southwark Cathedral** is so picturesque that a picnic lunch, made up of spoils from the local markets, can easily roll into a lazy afternoon. Many a star-crossed lover has trod the ancient boards of the nearby **Shakespeare's Globe**, but it's the remains of the **Rose Theatre** (or a replica of, belonging to Dame Judi Dench) that featured in the award-winning film *Shakespeare in Love* in which Gwyneth Paltrow's Viola falls for Joseph Fiennes' bard.

A walk along the Thames leads past the permanently moored **HMS Belfast**, which can be boarded from the footpath running from London Bridge to Tower Bridge and is home to one of WWII's better known tragic wartime romances (see **When Norman Met Eileen**, overleaf). Beyond Tower Bridge and More London, arguably the best named street in town, lies Terence Conran's **Blueprint Café**, where diners are handed signature blue binoculars with which to watch the world below.

The riverside towards Rotherhithe is a thing of beauty, but it was thanks to one local activist that there is access to it at all; when Conran was redeveloping Butler's Wharf in the 1980s, one woman wanted to ensure that local people and the general public could walk freely along the south bank of the Thames. The developers wanted to restrict such movement – so that the space could be exploited for cafés and restaurants. The woman won, and the alleyway that leads down to the river is named after her: Maggie Blake's Cause. For an ale and a river view, **The Mayflower**, a ye olde worlde-style pub, is a great stop-off.

Bermondsey Street is an ode to local entrepreneurism: **José** and **Pizarro**, the namesake restaurants for their Spanish chefs, are the upmarket choice and serve excellent sherry and tapas; at the other end of the street (in both senses) is **M.Manze** where the dish of choice is jellied eels and sarsaparilla, a fruit drink which was originally used to cure syphilis. Bonding over rancid foods is fine, but for the more traditionally romantic environs, Tooley Street's French-influenced restaurant **Magdalen** is run by husband and wife, James and Emma Faulks, whose brief to designers was 'no chrome, no fur and no plastic'. One of the less orthodox examples of entrepreneurism is **Holly and Lil**, the shop which sells 'collar couture' for the more sartorial pug; their bespoke collections have even adorned the necks of celebrities – Boss the Boxer, the star of *Tamara Drewe*, won the Palm Dog at Cannes Film Festival, sporting a Holly and Lil pirate collar. The Sunday roast at **The Garrison** is regularly voted by food critics and bloggers alike as London's best; booths at the back are a great cozy Sunday spot and can be booked in advance. There's also a cinema room, described as 'somewhere between garden shed and country cottage' and a table, number sixteen, which has drawers that, since the pub opened, have been slowly filling up with people's notes, doodles, confessions and full-blown stories.

Back on Bermondsey Square, the **Shortwave Cinema** is a charming independent picture house which shows art house and indie flicks after their release date – in case you missed them the first time. It also houses **Six Wines Eight**, a wine shop which only stocks forty-eight bottles of wine at a time – six wines in eight styles, each categorised by a colour and a three-word description (i.e. 'celebrate, bubble, pop' or 'intense, complex, elegant'). The wines are also all organic and biodynamic, no less. The pair who own the shop pride themselves on helping the more clueless drinker to choose the right bottle.

WHEN NORMAN MET EILEEN

Norman Battersby met Eileen Smith in 1944 while on leave in Essex from his job as a gunner in the Royal Navy. The two began a brief but intense affair, mostly through a series of letters that are still in existence. The first few are chatty and informal, set eerily against the backdrop of the war: 'Oh! Heck. The siren has just gone off again for the umpteenth time' and 'one of the girls said she would buy me a mascot for my bike. Guess what it turned out to be – nothing but a little sailor which is now a good favourite with all at the office'.

The two began to fall in love, despite having only intermittent moments together, and on one particular weekend, Norman proposed to Eileen, intending to send a formal letter to her parents shortly after. But before he could he received a letter from her mother, informing him that Eileen had been killed in a car accident. 'She rather liked you Norman as you had such fun at Ifracombe. She would have liked me to write to you.' There remains a deep tragic irony to the fact that Norman went on to survive a series of life-threatening events serving in the Navy, including on HMS *Belfast*, yet had lost his fiancée in a freak accident.

FROM SALT BEEF ON RYE TO GREAT BALLS OF FIRE

. . . .

Brick Lane

Calling all urbanites, artists and historians: for a date that marries ye olde London to contemporary art's hipster scene, trendy Hoxton to Bangladeshi London, head to Brick Lane. Its refusal to bear any tag is epitomised by the **Brick Lane Mosque**, formerly a synagogue and before that, a church.

The industrial **Beigel Bake** is the ideal meeting point, on the corner of Bethnal Green Road, a brunch-time Mecca for binmen and gallery owners alike. Legendary graffiti artists set the scene, with tags from Banksy, D*Face and Ben Eine within spitting distance. The 'salt beef on rye' is favoured by those with local knowledge: the most famous customer is Mick Taylor, who has been sitting outside the bakery for nearly fifty years. Known as the Sartorialist of Brick Lane, Taylor has become famous for his debonair style.

There's hardly a shortage of vintage shops on and around Brick Lane, but two very different collections run by two very different couples (see **Vintage Lovers**, p92) are worth the amble up Bacon Street. Cheshire Street has attracted an ever-increasing number of design shops that beckon the aesthete with their unusual homewares, artworks and vintage clothes. It's unlikely that this would have fitted the interior design tastes of the erstwhile owners of the nearby **Carpenter's Arms**. The notorious Kray twins bought the pub for their mother, who used to hold court in it at weekends, and, at one point, ominously replaced the bar counter with a coffin lid.

Back on Brick Lane, a huge cylindrical tower keeps watch over the hipsters and tourists, the familiar chimney of the **Old Truman Brewery**, whose clock

house has been in operation since the eighteenth century. Back then, it was London's largest brewery; today, it hosts businesses and events as diverse as The Great Spitalfields Pancake Race, Fashion East, the London Coffee Festival, The London Tattoo Convention, a drive-in cinema, and urban games competitions.

Across the road is Dray Walk, which on weekends bustles with Shoreditch trendies sitting at long tables clutching flat whites, newspapers and their bounty from any of the shops along what is known locally as 'the Strip'. At one point, the dot-com boom in east London almost had Brick Lane renamed 'Click Lane', but when the bubble burst, a host of craft fairs, exhibitions and night clubs appeared in its place, including the popular club and music venue **93 Feet East** and the **All Star Lanes** bowling alley. The curry houses lining Brick Lane may be a bold choice for a first date but sharing a platter at **Preem** or bringing your own bubbly at **Aladin** adds romantic spice. HRH Prince Charles endorsed the latter, if you really need persuading.

Across Commercial Road from the end of Brick Lane you will find the **Old Spitalfields Market**, London's oldest market: antiques on Thursdays, fashion on Fridays, with a record fair on the first and third Friday of the month where evangelical record sellers peddle their carefully catalogued boxes of old vinyl. On Saturdays it's vintage and on Sundays 'a little bit of everything'. If the stalls aren't good enough, the old market is now surrounded by the new: independent restaurants and shops including the celebrated **St John Bread and Wine** for carnivores, and **Montezuma's** where Great Balls of Fire (spiced chocolate caramel balls) satisfy sweet teeth. In the market square, couples can take free taster classes in tango with Argentinian couple René and Hiba on a warm summer evening.

Among the back streets of Spitalfields, a thriving community of sculptors, painters and drawers live, drink and commune. At the epicentre of this community, in every sense, is **The Golden Heart** pub on Commercial Street, run by legendary landlady Sandra, known as the Queen of the Arts Scene, and her husband Dennis for thirty years until his death in 2009. One typical anecdote involves her inviting Elton John's dancers back to the pub after an event in the West End to dance on the bar in full costume.

VINTAGE LOVERS

Bacon Street is home to two couples who have created their own unique collections of furniture, bric-a-brac and clothes from bygone eras. In fact, Des and Lorraine of **Des and Lorraine's Junk Shop** call it just that – junk. Des is a true collector – some of the pieces are from his own childhood and not even for sale. The deciding factor on acquiring his curios – from musical instruments to giant potato peelers – is whether they look good hanging from the roof, and the result is a cornucopia of stuff, a mesmerising other-worldly collection dangling out of the gloom. The prize trophy is arguably the mummified mermaid in a glass tank – apparently verified by carbon dating as over 200 years old.

This dark and strange pile is a far cry from Des and Lorraine's neighbours, Jess and Oli. In an age where anyone with a vaguely old T-shirt can open a vintage store, Jess and Oli's **Vintage Emporium** is the real deal. This is by no means a random collection – each item has been carefully selected and displayed, from the fully-functioning Bakelite telephone hanging on the wall to the cluster of antique tables and chairs and the reassuringly expensive (because they're worth it) vintage clothes downstairs. The specificity is its era – everything inside dates from between the Victorian era and the 1950s, and the *pièce de résistance* is the Victorian-style tea rooms where a range of teas, cakes and goodies (all true to period) are served on dainty china. At night you might enter to find singers, dancers and even the odd nude muse, as the store plays host to life drawing, ballet classes and open mic nights.

PLACES TO WATCH THE WORLD GO BY

Whether for people-watching, picnicking
or just looking up at the sky, take a spontaneous
trip to some of these special spots with
no advance planning required …

Rhizotron and Xstrata Treetop Walkway

Kew Gardens, TW9 3AB

From the designers of the London Eye, this spectacular highline stands at eighteen metres tall, and guides visitors around Kew Gardens' crowns of lime, sweet chestnut and oak trees.

Thames Barrier

1 Unity Way, SE18 5NJ

Perhaps the most peaceful spot in London. The landscape here may be stark and industrial but when you reach the barrier itself, its huge steel gates rising from the Thames are quite breathtaking, and there are stunning gardens from which to admire the view.

Frank's Café

10th Floor, Peckham multi-storey car park, 95a Rye Lane, SE15 4ST

The top of a multi-storey car park might not be everyone's idea of a date night, but this bar and gallery space has become the place for artists and fine young things to see – the view is quite spectacular – and be seen.

The Emirates Air Line

Greenwich Peninsula and Royal Docks, SE10

The Emirates Air Line, the first cable car over the Thames, linking the O2 Arena to Royal Docks, opened to the public in summer 2012, just in time for the Olympics. London's mayor, Boris Johnson, launched it, declaring that his first trip made him feel like the Russian cosmonaut Yuri Gagarin.

Alexandra Park

N22 7AY

With its sweeping views over London, and a farmers' market on site, this is the ideal spot for a Saturday picnic in north London.

Tate Modern Restaurant

Tate Modern, Bankside, SE1 9TG

The view from the restaurant on the seventh floor is a work of art in itself – with postcard-perfect views from the Gherkin to St Paul's.

Barge Walk

Hampton Court, KT8 9AV

Hugging the curve of the river from Hampton Court Bridge to Kingston is a tree-lined stroll, replete with clusters of anglers, swans, rowers and vine-covered walls. Halfway along you'll find a former waterworks, where water cascades from pipes into the river, delightfully named Seething Wells.

Café Boheme

13 Old Compton Street, W1D 5JQ

Having a bowl of moules marinières while sitting outside at one of the pavement tables is one of the best ways to while away an afternoon of people-watching amid the hustle and bustle of Soho, at the epicentre of London's gay community.

London Beaches

South Bank, SE1

When the tide of the Thames is low, the beaches of the South Bank are sometimes used for late-night parties, and even picnics. Make sure you bring a waterproof blanket.

Up at The O2

The O2, SE10 0DX

Not recommended for those with a fear of heights, but if you can stomach the walk across the dome of the O2 on a walkway suspended between two masts, the views from the observation platform at the end are unrivalled.

FROM CAGED BIRDS
TO POTTED PIGS

. . . .

Columbia Road

If there's ever a reason to start Sunday with the dawn, **Columbia Road Flower Market** is it. Almost before the sun is up, the market's legendary hawkers are in full flow, each stall with its own flowers, plants and herbs, and often its own unique patter: 'Treat your lady with an orchid! She deserves it.' 'Daffs! Daffs!' With its joyous cacophony of sounds, colours and smells it's impossible not to feel transported to the Victorian roots from which the market sprang. Even the name of the pub at the corner of the street, **The Birdcage**, recalls the erstwhile fashion for caged songbirds. Charles Dickens was deeply involved with the development of the area, but the woman who made it all happen is lesser known: Angela Burdett-Coutts, the granddaughter of the Coutts Bank founder (see **A Legacy of Flowers**, p107).

Round the corner, the photographer Seamus Ryan hosts the now-famous **Sunday Shoots** at his Ezra Street studio. He may have photographed some of the rich and famous – his Tom Stoppard portrait, for example, now hangs in the National Portrait Gallery – but on Sundays, he will photograph everyone and anyone who stops by to participate (without charge). The energy of the studio is completely unique to the moment – sometimes it might be an old man and his dog shyly glancing at the lens; at other times, entire families and groups of friends cram into the studio, shouting encouragement to each other as they pose for the camera. It's a rare opportunity to have a professional immortalise your Sunday – your photo might even form part of Ryan's stylish movie compilations, such as the charming HUG montage.

There's another Ryan in town, but he's no relation. Rob Ryan is also a highly celebrated artist, who has reinvented the forgotten art of papercutting. Paul Smith described him as a 'realistic romantic' which expresses perfectly the way that Ryan captures the quotidian in a beautiful and original style (although the world and his craft-loving wife is now trying to copy him). **Ryantown** is his shop on Columbia Road, which is where you'll find his very latest designs before they filter into other shops across the capital. And if ultra-affordable miniature artworks appeal, Ryan's screen-printed tiles, fired nearby in his studio's kiln, line the mantelpiece. Suck and chew on rhubarb-and-custard boiled sweets or paper-wrapped chocolate fags from nearby **Suck and Chew** as you decide how many tiles to buy at the very reasonable £24 price tag. At number 146A you'll find another artist, Nathan Hanford, aka **Three Letter Man**, whose studio lies hidden up a rickety staircase, where Hanford works from the windowsill, creating exquisite hand-embroidered artwork. He describes his works as 'meditations … tattoos for those afraid of needle pricks', and they are certainly unlike anything you will have seen before.

Arms filled with flowers, it's time to take a load off, and Columbia Road has plenty on offer to help you unwind. Ezra Street's **Printers and Stationers** is an off-licence with a difference; at the back is a small bar area, buried among rickety furniture, piles of books and hunting trophies, where you can buy either by the glass or by the bottle at a small mark-up. **Brawn**, from the chefs that brought you Terroirs in central London, is named after a peasant dish of potted pig's head (much tastier than it sounds). The menu divides into Taste Tickler, Pig, Cold, Hot and Pudding & Cheese. Back on Ezra Street you'll find Colchester oysters on sale on the table outside **Jones Dairy**, an old-fashioned grocer housed in a former milking shed – inside you can still see signs of the old working dairy.

Emma and Benito, the owners of **Campania Gastronomia** at the other end of Columbia Road, are from the Campania region of Italy and, consequently, the fashionable and bustling restaurant (only open during the daytime) feels a bit like you're eating in their Italian villa. Diners compete for space with wine racks that stretch to the ceiling and overhanging legs of ham, and the antipasti is delicious.

If the brunching frenzy becomes too much, a short walk away, past Hackney City Farm, past the fledgling **Goldsmith Row book market** and, on a Saturday, through Broadway Market, is London's trendiest picnicking spot – London Fields. There are ping-pong tables and boules pits, but mostly, just lots of fixies (fixed-gear bicycles) and onesies (all-in-ones), the hallmarks of the local hipster community. The recently refurbished Lido is one of London's most beautiful places to swim and makes for a refreshing dip on a hot day; otherwise just graze and people-watch until the sun goes down.

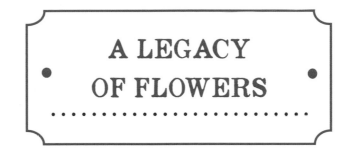

A LEGACY
OF FLOWERS

Angela Burdett-Coutts's life was dramatically altered in 1837 when she received an endowment of £3 million from her grandfather, Thomas Coutts, making her England's richest woman and extremely popular all of a sudden. Although she wasn't averse to a lavish party, counting Dickens and even Queen Victoria among her guests, her real passion was philanthropy. She supported all manner of initiatives, but one of her tours de force was to help found the Columbia Market Buildings, the design of which – a grand, covered 400-stall market in the style of a French Gothic cathedral – she had the advice of Dickens to thank. The end of her life was shrouded in scandal, with the deluge of proposals finally silenced when, at the age of sixty-seven, she decided to marry her twenty-seven-year-old American secretary. A stipulation in her grandfather's will that she must never marry a foreigner meant that she fought fiercely with her sister over the remaining endowment. However, right until she died, Angela was giving her money away, and the weekly eruption of pineapple sage, catmint, bamboo and cut flowers is her lasting legacy.

FROM HUGO'S TO LEXI'S

· ·

Queen's Park and Kensal Rise

Tucked unassumingly away from the busier Salusbury Road down a cobbled mews street in Queen's Park and flanked on either side by local businesses and artist studios lies **Hugo's**, a favourite spot with locals for a brunch-time Bloody Mary, sat at one of their old church pews. By night, the candles come out and they even have jazz on a Sunday, but for some northwest London laziness it's a fine way to start your day.

Another Sunday morning fixture in the area is the **Queen's Park Farmers' Market**, based at Salusbury Road Primary School. As can be expected from London farmers' markets, there is the inevitable plethora of biodynamically grown vegetables and 'hot from the pan' organic sausages, pricey but worth it. The atmosphere, especially when the sun is out, is infectious, and the lamb burgers unmissable. Round the corner is

The Salusbury pub where all the beautiful, young hipsters congregate to munch on pizza slices and drink red wine, bags full of trendy clothes from local boutique **Iris** under one arm and poetry from **Queen's Park Books** under the other. There is an adjoining enoteca offering wine-tasting and it's the ideal place to pick up a bottle or two to complete your picnic.

Queen's Park itself is a haven of gentle joggers doing laps of the thirty-acre site, throngs of children at the petting zoo (famous for its crazy rabbits), picnicking couples and weekend sporty types competing on its tennis courts, pitch and putt golf course and petanque/boules court. The park was built as the temporary site for the 1879 Royal Agricultural Society Show, with a working dairy, a cohort of agricultural machinery and a farmyard of animals. The show ran at a loss and moved to a new

permanent site but it drew attention to the area and a public campaign ran to ensure some green space was retained in the face of an ever-expanding London. The park was opened in 1886 in honour of Queen Victoria, and later became the home of the famous Queen's Park Rangers football team, before they moved to Loftus Road in White City.

On the other side of the park, **Kensal Green Cemetery** was the very first of the Magnificent Seven garden-style cemeteries from which the likes of Highgate Cemetery followed suit (see p202). When the cemetery first opened, not being buried in a churchyard was pretty controversial, but, once the Duke of Sussex had made his bed there, the cemetery became 'the place' to be interred. The best way to discover its inhabitants, both living (thirty-three species of bird and other wildlife) and dead, is

one of the Sunday guided tours – all given by volunteers who add their own twist and specialised knowledge. In the catacombs there are even 150-year-old coffins with their red velvet coverings intact. VIP graves to look out for include those of authors Wilkie Collins, William Makepeace Thackeray and playwright Harold Pinter. But quite apart from the history, the canal and grounds make it a near paradise to spend a lazy afternoon walking through.

For a more lively version of heaven, **Paradise by Way of Kensal Green** boasts a superb combination of Sunday newspapers, Yorkshire pudding and a resident DJ playing old 45s and rare bootlegs as part of the aptly named Sunday Recovery Sessions. On other nights there is an array of entertainment – comedy, life drawing of burlesque models, and Sophie Dahl even had her birthday here, with Jade Jagger on the decks as DJ. A more

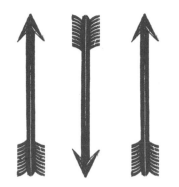

conventionally romantic alternative is **Ida** on the corner of Kilburn Lane, run by husband and wife Avi and Simonetta Reichenbach who have dedicated their lives to pasta and named their restaurant after Avi's mother, who taught him to cook. The pasta is made in-house, needless to say – you can even get involved with some pasta-making yourself on one of their excellent courses.

Chamberlayne Road, hailed by *Vogue* as the hippest street in Europe, earns its title with an array of vintage furniture and curiosity shops (Howie & Belle and Circus Antiques), gastropubs (The Chamberlayne and William IV) and **The Shop**, full of outrageous trendiness, cocktails served in milk bottles and even a

pulled pork southern-style food night. **Scarlet and Violet** is the favourite florist of Nigella Lawson and Louis Vuitton, among many others, and its Christmas wreaths are worth crossing London for.

Lazy days are best finished with a trip to the movies and just up Chamberlayne Road is the UK's first social enterprise, independent, boutique digital cinema, **The Lexi**, converted from Kensal Rise's Constitutional Club. On the front wall is inscribed the adage, '**I AM CINEMA, LOVE ME**' (see overleaf), which the philanthropist founder (who signs her name Dreamer rather than Chief Executive) has made sure of with her loyal following to this very unique venue.

I AM CINEMA, LOVE ME

When Sally Wilton sold her corporate training venue business for £21 million, she and her fellow trustees set off to Stellenbosch, South Africa to get involved with the Lynedoch EcoVillage, staffed by passionate local volunteers. While they were out there, a bizarre micro tornado back in Kensal Rise summoned her home, and it was the community spirit in piecing the neighbourhood back together that inspired her to launch the Lexi Cinema, named after her daughter, Alex.

It's an intimate screening room of forty seats, but by no means amateur, with a heavyweight arena-tour sound system and a lighting installation by Eden Project's Bruce Munro. The cinema has attracted all manner of arts greats – from Nick Roeg to Bill Nighy – but it's the sense of intimacy and community engagement which sets it apart. Each film is personally introduced, sometimes by the stars themselves – Miranda Richardson, for example, read from Daphne du Maurier's *The Birds* before the screening of the same film – there are Q&As, but crucially, every penny of profit goes straight to Lynedoch EcoVillage, to which Sally first committed her support.

FROM AFTERNOON PICNICS TO TWILIGHT BARKING

·································

Primrose Hill

Primrose Hill has gained a reputation in recent years for hosting the so-called 'Primrose set', a cohort of wife-swapping, coke-sniffing celebrities photographed tottering home to their million-pound mansions past Sunday morning joggers. But it is still one of London's best lazy neighbourhoods, almost as if it has been designed for the Sunday hangover. With its stucco terraces and designer boutiques, Primrose Hill is nothing if not chichi, and there are no supermarkets, chain stores, McDonalds or even a Starbucks – this is the last bastion of independent, privately owned shops and cafés against the giants of consumerism. To wander past a bona fide fishmonger, **La Petite Poissonerie**, on one side and one of those iconic red telephone boxes on the other feels like you've stepped back in time, such is the integrity of this north London neighbourhood.

Before heading to the hill itself, the main stretch of shops, Gloucester Avenue, offers a unique selection of picnic goodies to accompany you. **Melrose and Morgan** not only do British classics from pies to savoury tarts, but they hand them over packaged up in a Melrose & Morgan cool bag, with just enough room for peanut butter cupcakes from **Primrose Hill Bakery** and freshly made green juice smoothies from **Yeomans** greengrocers. Primrose Hill itself is known as the Everest of London, for its unrivalled panoramic view of the city. There is something sacred about this spot – it allows you to climb a few metres above all of the mayhem and madness and reflect quietly. Perhaps for this reason it is

the long-held meeting place of British Druids for their first public ceremony of the year – the Autumn Equinox (Spring happens at Tower Hill and Summer at Stonehenge). Many north Londoners associate the view with the best place to flock on Bonfire Night – after all, there's no need for your own fireworks display if you've got a ringside seat to every show in town. This hill has been the source of inspiration for every kind of art form over the years (see **The view is so nice**, p119) – Samuel Pepys even planted Shakespeare's Tree on the hill in 1864 to commemorate his 300th anniversary; it died and was replaced a hundred years later.

If you don't have the energy for talking, let a local luminary hold court at **St Mary's** on Primrose Hill, which hosts Weekly Lectures every Wednesday evening during the summer months, with the opportunity to meet the speaker for a glass of wine afterwards. Past speakers (and speeches) include Alan Bennett on libraries, Diana Athill on ageing and David Aaronovitch on politics. From mind expansion to something for the body and soul, **TriYoga** offers three kinds of yoga: Gyrokinesis, supposedly like a 'hypnotic, breath-generated dance', Kundalini, 'the mother of all yogas', and Never-Too-Late Yoga for the old, stiff or unfit.

All lazy days need to include an unhurried and laid-back dinner and across the road from TriYoga is Britain's first vegetarian restaurant, **Manna**, whose *raison d'être* is to treat veggie cuisine like any other, putting paid to its bland reputation. **The Engineer**, when it first opened,

was one of the founding fathers of the London gastropub scene, and its wholly seasonal food supplied, unsurprisingly, by small independent producers. For a more old-school feel, **Queens** was Kingsley Amis' favourite boozer and crucially is happy to welcome dogs – a prerequisite for one of London's most prolific dog-owning communities. Take note: to jog on Primrose Hill without a canine companion is almost seen as unsociable.

As day fades into night, three of the area's most legendary restaurants open their doors for ever-thriving trade – the pretty little French **Odette**, the Greek restaurant **Lemonia** and the Russian **Trojka**, which is made all the more authentic on Friday and Saturday nights by the sound of live Russian music.

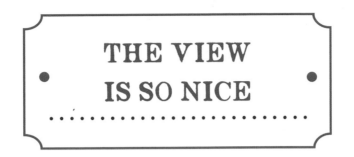

THE VIEW IS SO NICE

As far back as William Blake, Primrose Hill has triggered artists' imaginations – the poet-illustrator supposedly climbed the hill where he had conversations with the Spirit of the Sun, leading him to believe that this area would be the foundation for one of the pillars of the biblical New Jerusalem:

The fields from Islington to
  Marylebone
To Primrose Hill and Saint John's Wood
Were builded over with pillars of gold
And there Jerusalem's pillars stood.

Dodie Smith used Primrose Hill as the setting in her iconic children's book *The Hundred and One Dalmatians* for Pongo's 'Twilight Bark', the dogs' 'song' through which the Dalmatian puppies are rescued from Cruella de Vil. And it has continued to inspire songs and singers ever since, including the likes of Red Hot Chilli Peppers, Paul McCartney, Madness and Oasis, whose famous *Wonderwall* cover, the black-and-white photo of a girl shown through a frame, was shot here.

In 2001, Damon Albarn, of rival Britpop band Blur, was strolling through Primrose Hill with his bandmate Graham Coxon, debating whether or not the group should stay together. As they talked, they came across a large splash of graffiti written across the pathway with the words 'The view is so nice', lyrics from Blur's hit song 'For Tomorrow'. It was as clear a sign as they could have hoped for that they should keep making music together. The words, though worn and faded now, can still just about be made out, although the band itself, of course, did eventually split up.

FROM DRESSING GOWNS
TO BEACH BLANKETS

· ·

Notting Hill

The northern end of the two-mile-long **Portobello Road Market** is the place to start your Notting Hill walk, with fewer Italian tourists, and stalls piled high with second-hand clothes, jewellery, books and music spilling out from underneath the Westway. But this isn't just flea market territory – it has also become a hotspot for cutting-edge designers, with the likes of retro underwear specialists **What Katie Did** selling their 1950s-inspired bullet bras. Even some upmarket designer stores have set up stalls here, so racks of Myla and Paul Smith brush up against piles of 'Kelvin Kleins'. Locals in the know head away from the crowds towards Golborne Road, where you can unearth interior treasures at **Ollie & Bow**, **Les Couilles du Chien** and **Kokon to Zai**. Back on the main drag, Portobello market continues in the direction of Notting Hill past a

cacophony of irresistible smells and tastes, with paella, churros, crêpes and falafel stalls all competing to serve your midday snack. The UK's first ever electric cinema opened halfway down the road, now **The Electric**, both a cinema and a member's club, with special rates on Electric Sundays. On the final stretch of the market lie some of the richest antique treasure troves in London – the smell of history seems to rise from the labyrinth of furniture and first-edition books.

The perfect place to escape the crowds is the **Chaya Teahouse** on St Luke's Road, run by the disarmingly courteous Pei Wang on Saturdays and Sundays (see **A Pause Button**, p124), for which it is essential to reserve in advance. An intimate ground-floor studio is filled with no more than ten beautifully carved wooden tables.

WHOLE CAKES AVAILABLE

There is a hush about the place, broken only by Wang's own gentle enquiries and, when asked, his elaborations on his favourite subject. To accompany the huge array of unusual teas are exotic patisseries such as mango-seed cake and yuzu meringue drops and tea savouries such as the intriguing lo mai fan – lotus-leaf rice parcel.

Westbourne Grove is the right place to maintain Pei Wang's infusion of calm with the chance to pamper and stock up on cashmere at **Brora** or body lotions and potions at **Aesop**. This is organic central – with **Tom's Deli** the destination for a posh full English and a deli with an international twist, or **Daylesford Organic**, which claims to bring the taste of the Gloucestershire countryside to Notting Hill.

Just when the walking gets too much, the ideal lazy end to the afternoon looms into sight in the shape of **Porchester Spa**, on the corner of Queensway and Porchester Road. Open on Sunday afternoons between 4 and 10 to couples only (of any gender combination), the labyrinthine interior is an art deco cauldron of green- and white-tiled walls and nymph-like statues that beckon to the lower quarters. The main concourse is a hazy café, where the windows are steamed up and clientele lounge in dressing gowns and flip-flops and play cards at round aluminium tables. The more energetic can get their lengths in next door in the large swimming pool underneath vast vaulted ceilings, but down white marble steps, you'll find a maze of steam rooms, Jacuzzis, saunas, Turkish hot rooms and treatment rooms. This is no fancy, fluffy-white-towel affair – there is an air of ancient practice about the place which, while a bit rough around the edges, is intoxicating and sexy.

Pummelled and steamed, it's a stone's throw in any direction for the restaurant or theatre in which to while away the evening. Evoking a sense of fairy tale with its different-sized rooms interconnected by tunnels, walkways and bridges, **Beach Blanket Babylon** does cocktails and dinner, best eaten in one of their turrets. Hereford Road has plenty to offer; at one end, **The Print Room** sees a fifties warehouse now converted into a flexible theatre space, often commended for its transformative and radical redesigns. At no. 4, **Inaho** offers authentic Japanese cuisine to twenty tightly packed tables.

A PAUSE BUTTON

Formerly a data manager, Pei Wang left his job for something more sensory, a job which involved his hands but, more importantly, to celebrate a ritual that he believes is a vital part of everyone's life – that of making and drinking tea. For Wang, the tea ceremony represents a moment in the day when everything else can be put on hold – a focusing on the different parts of the process: the boiling of water, the heating of various pots and cups, the specific timing of infusion.

In his online blog, Teahouse Stirrings, Wang outlines his own philosophies on tea-drinking and the history of the myriad types of tea around the world. For example, Oolong tea came about after a perspiring farmer left his tea leaves in his backpack and they began to oxidise, giving off a new aroma that the farmer had never experienced before. Now the word 'oolong' (literally 'black dragon') is used by the Chinese to mean any kind of error. Wang believes that in the modern day, it is critical to take more time to live in the present – that we are naturally inclined towards the future or distracted by emails, phone calls and the paraphernalia of modern life that takes us away from the moment. And for Wang, it is in making and drinking tea that this crucial pausing can take place.

BRILLIANT BRUNCHES

The ten best spots to cure a hangover, read the papers, and have a breakfast fit for kings.

Hawksmoor

157 Commercial Street, E1 6BJ

The best brunch for meat lovers, famed for its steaks aged for thirty-five days. It's hard to resist the sound – and taste – of the cornflake-milk milkshake. The cornflakes are soaked in milk overnight, and then the milk is used (without any cornflakes) to make the ice cream for the shake.

Regency Café

17–19 Regency Street, SW1P 4BY

This art deco café featured in the film *Layer Cake*, and does the best comfort food in town, with its famous fry-up a mere £5.50.

Maria's Market Café

• •

8 Southwark Street, Borough Market,
SE1 1TL

Maria Moruzzi started work aged
seven in her parents' café on nearby
Park Street. She has been in the
business ever since, attracting locals
to her greasy spoon with her now
world-famous bubble & squeak.

Automat

• •

33 Dover Street, W1S 4NF

Mayfair majesty meets all-American
diner at this extremely popular
brunch destination. Sitting in one
of their 'railway carriage' booths,
you'll find a menu full of American
treats like the soft shell crab 'Po Boy'
sandwich with fries.

Banners

• •

21 Park Road, N8 8TE

A Crouch End institution, serving
enormous breakfasts, with or without
the Caribbean influence that it's
famous for. If you do go for a Jamaican
breakfast, it's served with spicy beans,
hash browns and ackee. Well worth
the trip even if you are not a local –
perhaps before a visit to nearby
Alexandra Palace.

Lowry & Baker

• •

339 Portobello Road, W10 5SA

Since opening in 2010, this one-room
café has become a local mainstay, with
its attention to detail and delicious
menu, inspired daily by the produce on
offer at Portobello Market.

Lantana

• • • • • • • • • • • • • • • • • • • •

13 Charlotte Place, W1T 1SN

Brunch is considered as important to Australians as afternoon tea is to the British, and Lantana shows us how it's done. Menu highlights include corn fritters and flat whites.

The Modern Pantry

• • • • • • • • • • • • • • • • • • •

47–48 St John's Square, EC1V 4JJ

Classy without being too expensive, with an outside courtyard in spring, Modern Pantry does British brunch with a twist – like ricotta pancakes served with poached rhubarb and crème fraîche, or coconut and cassava waffles.

The Riding House Café

• • • • • • • • • • • • • • • • • • • •

43–51 Great Titchfield Street, W1W 7PQ

Brunch specials from fortifying Bircher muesli to chorizo hash browns served against a backdrop of eclectic reclaimed and bespoke furniture. A stone's throw from the chaos of Oxford Street, yet it still feels off the beaten track.

Bill's

• • • • • • • • • • • • • • • • • • • •

9 White Lion Street, N1 9PD

Brighton's favourite brunch spot arrived in London in 2012, offering an eco-friendly mix of food market, deli and brunch spot inspired by seasonal British produce.

FROM GAUGUIN'S NUDE
TO FREUD'S ICE CREAM

. . . .

Somerset House and Aldwych

The splendid courtyard in front of **Somerset House** has been variously filled with 10,000 ceramic daffodils, a circle of twelve enormous bronze animal heads sculpted by Chinese artist Ai Weiwei, and revellers dancing to dance music beneath the night sky. It's hard to believe that until the late 1990s, the space was used as a car park for civil servants working for the Inland Revenue.

But now one of London's most spectacular eighteenth-century buildings has become a contemporary cultural hub that genuinely has something for everyone. The courtyard is its beating heart, hosting in winter what Harper's Bazaar describes as 'London's most glamorous ice rink', under the boughs of a Christmas tree designed by Tiffany & Co, and in summer shooting fifty-five jets of water from its belly, to the delight of the children (and adults) who play among them.

Armed with pizzas from the Pizza Express next door, duvets, pillows and rugs, the highlight of the Somerset House calendar is the summer screenings that cast a sleepover spell on the strangely intimate gathering of 2,000 viewers. As the light fades, bottles are uncorked, picnic blankets unfurled, and all eyes turn to the vast screen, suspended in front of walls dramatically illuminated in purple. Films shown are mainly old favourites, but the courtyard also hosts the occasional premiere for new work by the likes of Pedro Almodovar (who now holds all his UK premieres there) and the gulls that traverse the beams of light in the sky above.

But the courtyard is by no means the only draw to this historic building – the **Courtauld Gallery** is perhaps the most perfect art collection in London. Unlike most other galleries in the capital, the Courtauld is rarely crowded and also has a small window of free entry for those with the luxury of time on a Monday morning. The gallery walls are filled with masters, predominantly Impressionist and post-Impressionist art, but the collection also boasts works from the early Renaissance right through to the twentieth century. It's the fact that some of Degas', Van Gogh's and Manet's masterpieces are permanently housed in such an intimate setting that makes the Courtauld so unique. This quality is best exploited through a private tour for two pre-booked through **Art History Tours**, where qualified art historians guide you through a series of heroic, humble, strange, sad and often hilarious stories. According to a recent poll, the painting to look out for is Paul Gauguin's *Nevermore* (see **New Romantics**, overleaf).

For cocktails afterwards, the art deco **American Bar** in The Savoy Hotel is home to some of the top mixologists in the country and the pianissimo sounds of Burt Bacharach and Cole Porter. In 1903 Ada Coleman took over the running of the bar as the first and only female head bartender at The Savoy. Her signature drink, the Hanky Panky (Bombay Sapphire gin, Italian vermouth and Fernet Branca) was created especially for the Edwardian actor Sir Charles Hawtrey, after he came in and exclaimed, 'Coley, I am tired. Give me something with a bit of punch in it.'

Recently opened, **The Delaunay**, from the men who brought us The Wolseley, is the new place to eat; its German-influenced menu features an array of wieners (that's right) and an ice cream called the Lucien, after the late painter Lucien Freud who ate at The Wolseley every single day.

NEW ROMANTICS

Paul Gauguin's *Nevermore* was recently voted the most romantic painting in the UK. It features a nude Tahitian girl reclining on a bed in the foreground, against the backdrop of a raven on a ledge and two figures in conversation. The painting was chosen in contrast to the chocolate-box concept of romance that has taken precedent in modern times – the panellist who chose the painting, artist and critic Matthew Collings, described his understanding of the word: 'For me the word "romantic" in a painting context means feeling. It has nothing to do with subject matter.'

Gauguin sought to fill the picture with mystery and ambiguity, and in his words, 'to suggest a certain long-lost barbarian luxury'. The girl's eyes are open but she doesn't look at us. Are the raven (a reference to the Edgar Allen Poe poem from which the painting's title comes) and the figures real or just figments of her imagination?

Unlike Manet's *Olympia*, which this painting mimics, Gauguin wasn't interested in realism or a literal sense of romance. His use of bright and smouldering colours, his distorted perspectives and heightened sense of imagination are what appeals to the viewer, suggesting that romance is really about the undefinable and the limitless.

FROM IRISH GIANTS TO BLEEDING HEARTS

. . . .

Lincoln's Inn Fields

Lincoln's Inn Fields, just off the busy Kingsway, is London's legal heartland; men and women in formal gowns stride out of towering doorways and into tiny alleyways that spill onto Oxbridge-style courtyard gardens. Picnicking on the Fields under the spring blossom feels like stepping back in time. This may be the largest public square in London but behind its grand eighteenth-century façades lie some of the capital's most intimate secrets and historical curiosities.

The east boundary of the square, with its collection of old buildings, is the place to begin. Lincoln's Inn itself was the starting point for some of literature's greatest works; it inspired Dickens' scabrous attack on the English legal system in *Bleak House*, and the first ever performance of Shakespeare's *A Midsummer Night's*

Dream took place in its garden. The Lincoln's Inn Chapel was the drop-in and drop-off clinic of the Georgian era for mothers too poor to look after their newborn babies. Every child was then officially adopted by the chapel, cared for until adulthood, and all children were given the surname Lincoln. The Ostler's Hut is the smallest listed building in London – it was built in 1860 for the man attending to law students' horses, but with the advent of the motor car a few years later, he was soon out of a job and the building was never used again.

For a less romantic but more macabre detour, the **Hunterian Museum**, on the south side of the square, houses row after row of medical curiosities, exhibited in glass jars spread over two floors. The collection was put together by eighteenth-century surgeon

John Hunter – clearly his ghoulish preoccupation ran in the family, as the Hunterian in Glasgow was set up by his brother William. Babies and foetuses have been pickled for posterity, and hernias float in jars next to diseased hearts. Hunter was a maverick, largely self-taught, and his impressive collection is so artfully arranged that even non-medics and the layman cannot fail to engage. The museum's mascot is the skeleton of 7 foot 7 inches giant Charles Byrne, whose exhibition in the Hunterian continues to attract controversy 230 years after his death (see **Irish Giant**, p140).

The Hunterian is often overlooked as it shares the square with a collection often claimed by Londoners and guidebooks alike as 'London's best kept secret' (where it is in fact pretty well known). On the north side of the square, **Sir John Soane's Museum** is an ingeniously designed rabbit warren of a place, with rooms of different sizes and on different levels, each managing to surprise and delight on discovery of yet more pictures, prints, books, objets, casts and sculptures crammed into every nook and cranny. The collection is housed in what was Soane's home and library, and the wonder of this collection is that Soane, Professor of Architecture at the Royal Academy, in no way attempted to distinguish between what was historically or aesthetically important – he just wanted it full of stuff and wanted his students to have easy access to it – which means that the massive 3,000-year-old sarcophagus of the Egyptian King, Seti I, is shown alongside a portrait of Mrs Soane's pet dog, Fanny. One family member who definitely doesn't feature is his son George, with

whom he had a lifelong spat; he even battled for a Private Act of Parliament to prevent the house and collection from falling into his son's hands.

If you look closely enough, there are masterpieces to be found – Turner, Hogarth, Canaletto – but it's the atmosphere of the whole house that will stay with you, and with it a real sense of its founder's character. The best way to see it is how Soane would have himself, by candlelight, which you can do on the first Tuesday of every month. Only sixty people are allowed in at a time, and it's first come, first served – so get there early if you don't want to be at the back of a very long queue.

Holborn, the area around Lincoln's Inn Fields, has some fairly uninspiring watering holes where the local legal community wash away the day's trials and tribulations, so it's worth seeking out the diamonds in the rough. In the direction of Covent Garden, **32 Great Queen Street**, from the men behind the much-feted gastropub The Anchor & Hope, does very good

food without shouting about it: from crab on toast or smoked mackerel for starters, to roast lamb or rump steak for main. Great Queen Street is also home to the controversial but beautiful Freemasons' Temple and shops displaying Masonic regalia. Masons in unfashionable dark suits surreptitiously enter the side door of the Temple carrying their ceremonial trowels and pinafores.

In the other direction, towards Farringdon, **Bleeding Heart Yard** is home to three French restaurants – the cosy **Tavern**, the mid-range **Bistro** and the white-tableclothed **Restaurant**. The sign outside the Tavern remembers the day when visitors to this eighteenth-century pub could get drunk for a penny and pass out on the straw free of charge. The yard itself is rumoured to have been named after the murder of Lady Elizabeth Hatton, her body found 'torn limb from limb, but with her heart still pumping blood'. As the *New Yorker* adroitly summed up, the restaurant is 'Bleeding Hard to find but worth it'.

THE IRISH GIANT

Born in the village of Littlebridge in Londonderry, as a young man Charles Byrne grew to a height of 7 foot 7 inches (by some accounts, an even greater 8 foot 2 inches), so tall that it was said he could light his pipe from gas streetlamps. He moved to London where he soon became the most talked-about curiosity in town, a fame that led to his amassing a small fortune. His fame was short-lived however; when his pocket was picked of his £700 life savings, Byrne was distraught, turned to drink and died shortly after, at the tender age of twenty-two.

A newspaper at the time of his death described the ensuing bun fight for his body: 'The whole tribe of surgeons put in a claim for the poor departed Irishman and surrounded his house just as harpooners would an enormous whale.' Byrne had been desperate not to have his corpse dissected and had requested emphatically that he be buried at sea. But, against his wishes, John Hunter took possession of the body by paying a bribe to one of Byrne's friends.

From a medical point of view, Hunter's actions have led directly to important discoveries – as recently as 2011, researchers determined the cause of Byrne's gigantism by extracting DNA from his teeth. But following this, a letter published in the *British Medical Journal* argued that all medical knowledge had now been gleaned and that Byrne should be granted his dying wish. The request was denied, but begs the question: if such a moral viewpoint was taken across the board, how many of London's museums would hold on to their main attractions?

FROM LITERARY LETTER WRITER TO BOTANICAL PORNOGRAPHER

Chelsea

These days, the likes of Mick Jagger take up residence in the wisteria-fronted riverside mansions of Chelsea's Cheyne Walk and the adjacent streets, but back in the Victorian era, it was the heart of the London literary set that lived there. Today, practically every other façade bears a blue plaque: overlooking the river at Number 16 lived co-inhabitants Dante Gabriel Rossetti and Algernon Charles Swinburne, just up the road from George Eliot at Number 4; Elizabeth Gaskell, at Number 93, was almost neighbours with James McNeill Whistler at Number 96; nearby Carlyle Mansions was home to Henry James; and A. A. Milne created his magical worlds at 13 Malford Street.

But at the time the real celebrities of the area were Scottish satirist and historian Thomas Carlyle and his wife Jane Welsh Carlyle, considered one of the nineteenth century's finest women of letters. Their complicated and ambiguous relationship was at the centre of constant gossip and speculation, long after their deaths (see **Love Letters**, p147). The house that they lived in, now known as **Carlyle's House**, at 24 Cheyne Row, has been immaculately and painstakingly restored with the same layout and even the same furniture, just as they had arranged it. After Carlyle's death, the house received new tenants who redecorated and sold off much of the furniture, but shortly after, friends and admirers of Carlyle took hold of the lease and, using a painting by Robert Tait of Carlyle, Jane and their dog Nero in the living room, they managed to track down most of the original furniture (then scattered across the world) through American auction houses and private collectors. The current custodian's sleight of hand is in the fact that the painting, which hangs in that very living room, now seems to feature a small part of itself.

The strange thing about the Carlyles is the disparity between their unrivalled social standing during their lifetimes and their relative obscurity now. Carlyle's followers were among the most esteemed: Charles Dickens described Carlyle as the man who most influenced him, dedicating *Hard Times* to him, and yet Carlyle described *The Pickwick Papers* as 'the lowest trash', *David Copperfield* as 'watery twaddle' and *Great Expectations* as 'that Pip nonsense'. George Eliot also declared his influence on her work – 'a grand favourite of mine'. Jane Welsh Carlyle knew a certain Mary Ann Evans but dismissed her on account

of her living out of wedlock with her lover. However, not knowing that she was the person behind the pseudonym George Eliot, she was a huge admirer of Eliot's first novel and wrote her a long fan letter, starting, 'Dear Sir, I have to thank you …'

Carlyle's influence even extended to the English language: 500 words and terms coined by him entered the *OED*, including 'hero-worship', 'environment', 'industralism' and the lesser-known 'natural supernaturalism'. No one knows exactly why their collective star faded after the Carlyle's deaths – some say that Carlyle's writings were in fact pretty inaccessible, but it may have been more to do with his focus on, and popularity with, the Germans, which proved less fashionable a few years later. Perhaps the real charm and appeal of the couple lay in their relationship with each other – his initial shyness brought out by her quick wit and humour, and their shared love of letters and language.

A few blocks away, another carefully cultivated and inspiring collection lies within the **Chelsea Physic Garden**, which has, since the eighteenth century, been used to develop and create new medicines through the understanding of herbs and plants. Locals come to sit near the oldest man-made rock gardens in Europe (some of which were once part of the Tower of London), seek shade behind the greenhouses (classified according to continent), or take a lesson in botany from the meticulous classification of every plant. Learn about the Botanical Pornographer, aka Carl Linnaeus, who in 1753 replaced the classification system (which described each plant in as many as thirteen words) with the now ubiquitous two-name system based not on the appearance of the plant, but on the arrangement of its sexual organs. Among the pharmaceutical beds, visitors are invited to spot the difference between the herb sweet cicely and its poisonous twin hemlock. Some of the more unusual residents include lady's mantle, aka *Alchemilla vulgaris*, supposedly a cure for 'such women or maids as have over great flagging breasts, causing them to grow less'.

The **Cheyne Walk Brasserie** with its pale olive décor is surprisingly calming and is the place to digest literary and botanical discoveries, along with Provençale fare served by (genuinely) French waiters and waitresses.

THOMAS·CARLYLE

·LIVED·AT·24·CHEYNE·ROW·1834—1881·

·THIS·TABLET·WAS·ERECTED·BY·THE·CARLYLE·SOCIETY·

CFA·VOYSEY·DELT   B·CRESWICK·Sc

LOVE LETTERS

In April 1909 an article was published in the *New York Times* entitled 'The Love Letters of Thomas Carlyle and Jane Welsh Solve Unique Literary Problem of Last Century'. The title alone goes to show the extent to which their relationship was discussed among the very highest and most influential circles. What was so curious was that in spite of the huge volume of love letters that they exchanged, over 9,000 in total, it was unclear whether they were actually lovers or merely friends, and whether they were happy or unhappy in their strange union. Their letters spoke of a changeable, passionate, at times sublimely romantic, at times miserably angry relationship. Indeed, Carlyle's biographer James Anthony Froude even claimed that the marriage remained unconsummated.

The pair's tortuous courtship is documented in their early letters. In one from Jane to Thomas in 1825, she warns: 'I love you, I have told you a hundred times … but I am not in love with you; that is to say, my love for you is not a passion which overclouds my judgement.' And yet, in the next letter, in September of the same year, everything has changed: 'Love! What I would give to have you here – within my arms, for one, for one moment!' The next year they were married.

FROM DULWICH PICTURE GALLERY TO THE HORNIMAN MUSEUM

. . . .

Dulwich and Forest Hill

Those who use their eyes obtain the most enjoyment and knowledge. Those who look but do not see go away no wiser than when they came.

Frederick Horniman

The **Dulwich Picture Gallery**, with its crimson walls and topsy-turvy crowded galleries, is as unlike a modern exhibition hall as you're likely to see. At 200 years old, it is also England's first public art gallery and one that continues to celebrate atmosphere over 'the done thing'. The exhibition spaces are converted from old almshouses and the paintings are hung close together to maintain a domestic, intimate feel.

It all began with a bequest by the eccentric dealer and collector Sir Francis Bourgeois, who went as far as bequeathing his own body as part of the deal. His mausoleum, lit by a moody *lumière mystérieuse* (mysterious light) created with tinted glass, was placed among the pictures. The tone of the gallery's pieces is of morbid romance – most notably, the anonymously painted *Judd Marriage*, where the happy couple make their vows with their hands atop a human skull, and Poussin's *Rinaldo and Armida* where the Saracen sorceress has enchanted the Christian warrior into a deep sleep in order to slay him, her hand stayed by love at the last minute. Despite its idiosyncrasies, the Dulwich Picture Gallery remains

defiantly forward-thinking and is one of the few flagship museums taking part in Google's Art Project, allowing virtual audiences to see paintings in minute detail using the same technology that allows us to zoom into streets with Google Earth.

For a leisurely romantic lunch the terraces at **Beauberry House**, a smart Grade II-listed manor, overlook the gorgeous Belair Park, or for something quicker, both Dulwich Village and nearby Lordship Lane are full of charming local cafés and delis.

On the corner of Dulwich Park, **London Recumbents** hire out adult tricycles to roam the surrounding parklands – tandems come in two forms: the co-pilot approach, where one cycles and the other sits up front, or the side-by-

side option. An empty plinth, where Barbara Hepworth's bronze *Two Forms (Divided Circle)* once stood, is a sad reminder of the infamous overnight theft by suspected scrap metal thieves.

At the top of Lordship Lane, another former private collection turned public is housed within the **Horniman Museum**, a completely unique array of anthropological curiosities and particularly remarkable taxidermy collection, set in sixteen acres of landscaped gardens. Standing sentry at the roadside entrance to the museum an eagle perches on the head of a girl who stands astride a bear – the characters making up a wooden totem, contributed by a Tingit native Alaskan, based on the legend of a girl who is punished for cursing the bear family by being deceived into

· ·

marrying one and bearing its children – half babies, half cubs.

Inside, the walls are lined with all manner of stuffed beast, from the rare Sunda pangolin to the extinct dodo (one of the few specimens that is *not* real, as you might expect) and the passenger pigeon. At the time of America's discovery by the Founding Fathers, there were three to five billion passenger pigeons in the States – Martha, thought to be the last, died in Cincinatti Zoo in 1914. On the balcony, one of the exhibits is known as the 'flashing bat', its open wings reminiscent of an old man's raincoat. Nearby the anableps, four-eyed fish, only have left- or right-handed copulatory organs, so finding a mate of the correct orientation is crucial.

Beyond its permanent residents, the museum curates a diverse programme of animal and anthropological exhibitions, ranging from the sublime to the ridiculous: In 2006, the museum launched a worldwide search for a huge stuffed polar bear which had been a documented favourite among the Victorian public but has not been seen since it was lent to Selfridges department store for a flamboyant Christmas window display sixty years ago. The Great White Bear exhibition was the result of an effort to photograph every taxidermied polar bear in the UK and showed bears in differently stuffed styles – including some particularly contorted and misshapen efforts before the 'realist' style of the mid-nineteenth century became the norm. But the undisputed emperor of the museum is the enormous Horniman walrus (see **@HornimanWalrus**, overleaf) who presides uncomfortably over the glass-fronted exhibits surrounding him. The museum is an odd blend of styles and interests, with one wing dedicated to human artefacts and the basement housing an aquarium. Reflecting the whims of its founder, the museum doesn't try to be complete or definitive in any area, and it is in this scattergun arrangement that its charm and attraction lies.

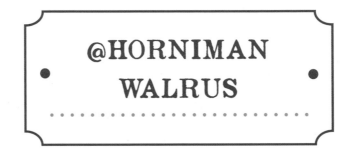

@HORNIMAN WALRUS

Now the Horniman Museum's best-loved exhibit, the Horniman walrus was brought to London by the Victorian hunter James Henry Hubbard, who collected it from Hudson Bay in Canada. When he handed it over to a taxidermist back in London, the stuffer in question, having never seen a live walrus, like most people of his day, had no idea that walruses have deep folds in their thick skin. Consequently, he did the logical thing and stuffed it to the brim, resulting in the gigantic, overweight creature that Horniman bought and which is now displayed as the museum's centrepiece. The lines where the folds should have been are still visible 140 years later. The walrus even has his own (unofficial) Twitter feed: @HornimanWalrus.

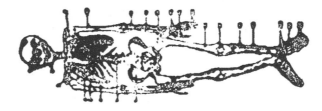

BOOKSHOPS FOR LOVERS

There is something inherently romantic about a small quiet space overflowing with books, where every nook holds the promise of immersion and escape. Here are the finest London bookshops in which to lose yourselves.

Lutyens and Rubinstein

21 Kensington Park Road, W11 2EU

Two literary agents set up this shop in which books rub spines with crockery and perfumes inspired by fiction – plates decorated with favourite book openings, and scents such as A Room with a View and In the Library, created by former taxi driver Christopher Brosius of CB I Hate Perfume.

Clerkenwell Tales

30 Exmouth Market, EC1R 4QE

David Nicholls' favourite London bookshop, known for stocking beautifully designed editions displayed immaculately and enticingly and for its book club, special events and book launches.

Magma

• •

8 Earlham Street, WC2H 9RY

Shelves of fashion, photography and design books arranged cover-out tower seven metres up to the ceiling. To encourage browsing, there are no signs or sections and each desirable edition has a plastic-covered sample copy for perusal.

Persephone Books

• •

59 Lamb's Conduit Street, WC1N 3NB

This fresh-flower-filled shop publishes and sells forgotten twentieth-century classics, mostly by women, with elegant grey covers and beautiful endpapers designed from vintage fabrics. Its engaging blog, The Persephone Post, gives readers a sense of the passion with which the shop's owner, Nicola Beauman, approaches her work.

Shepherds Bookbinders

• •

76 Rochester Row, SW1P 1JU

This specialist bindery hosts workshops in bookbinding, book restoration and box-making. Or simply watch the specialist bookbinders at work in the back of the shop and browse the stunning collection of special editions, Japanese papers, photo albums and boxes.

The Bookseller Crow On The Hill

• •

50 Westow Street, SE19 3AF

Run by knowledgeable and attentive couple Jonathan and Justine, and neatly summed up by Man Booker Prize-winner Yann Martel, who said: 'The mental space represented is as vast as the universe.' One of the few bookshops in London to stock American editions of books and will order them for you. Watch what you say when you visit – the owners tweet about their more amusing or absurd customer encounters.

The Bookshop

• • • • • • • • • • • • • • • • • • • •

1d Calton Avenue, SE21 7DE

Its owners Julian and Hazel seem to have read everything on the jam-packed shelves and will proffer capsule reviews from behind the counter. Plus it's open on Sundays, surely the best time for carefree browsing.

Heywood Hill

• • • • • • • • • • • • • • • • • • • •

10 Curzon Street, W1J 5HH

Selling antiquarian as well as new books, Heywood Hill is a shop with a fascinating history: when its owner was called to war in 1942, the shop was saved by the help of Nancy Mitford, who manned the shop with a group of friends. Look out for the shop's line in collected letters between friends and lovers.

Primrose Hill Bookshop

• • • • • • • • • • • • • • • • • • • •

134 Regent's Park Road, NW1 8XL

Jessica and Marek are voracious readers who make thoughtful recommendations. Their small but perfectly formed shop is laid out in a way that somehow makes finding an elusive book incredibly easy. They produce beautiful booklets at Christmas and in the summer, and have hosted the likes of Martin Amis, Ian McEwan and Doris Lessing at their intimate events.

Daunt Books

• • • • • • • • • • • • • • • • • • • •

83 Marylebone High Street, W1U 4QW

A beautiful Edwardian building with oak galleries and skylights, fragrant with binding glue and printing ink. In a nod to its genesis as a bookshop for travellers, the shop is arranged geographically, so that travel guides and phrasebooks sit alongside the fiction, poetry and non-fiction from each country. This makes for an original and inspiring browsing experience, especially if you are planning a holiday.

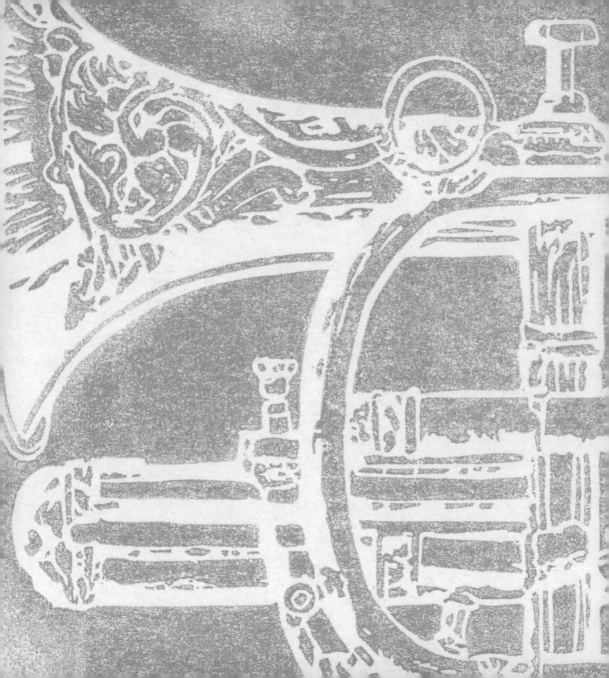

FROM LONDON ZOO TO OPEN AIR THEATRE

. . . .

Regent's Park

Camden Market, just around the corner from the Hawley Arms, an infamous boozer for notorious modern lovers including the late Amy Winehouse and Blake Fielder-Civil, and Kate Moss and Pete Doherty, is a high-octane, bustling jumpstart for an afternoon's ramble. Latex outfits or his 'n' hers tattoos are in abundance, but the less deviant deviation lies down the Regent's Canal towpath, past the Pirate Castle on the far bank, where kayaks, rowboats and even narrow boats float side by side.

As the canal winds its way past staggeringly beautiful homes on the edge of Regent's Park, the Snowdon Aviary looms into view, its spiky geometric architecture draped with netting to hold on to its residents: green peafowl, sacred ibis, cattle egrets and African grey-headed gulls – a feathered taster of the wonders of **London Zoo** (see **An Animal Microcosm of London**, p164).

In the spring, there is perhaps nowhere more romantic in London than **Queen Mary's Rose Garden**. The roses themselves are so evocative that, for Sylvia Plath, they became kings and queens of the surrounding rockeries in her poem dedicated to the garden. The ornamental ducks and carp complete the picture and, for growling stomachs, the smell of crispy bacon rolls and organic bangers from family-run **The Honest Sausage**, located at the Broad Walk off Chester Road, is irresistible.

As dusk falls, it is the **Regent's Park Open Air Theatre** that beckons the more intrepid theatre-goers for

performances under the open skies. Couples sip Pimm's and set up hampers on the picnic lawn, any time between May and September, as actors perform works ranging from George Gershwin to William Shakespeare. A particular treat is the late-night sessions with storytelling comic legend Daniel Kitson (of Crystal Palace's 66a Church Road), spellbinding his listeners with his delicious use of wordplay. The theatre celebrates work that finds a symbiosis between the piece and the surroundings in which it is performed – plays like *A Midsummer Night's Dream* and *Into the Woods* are obvious contenders, but for the less likely *Lord of the Flies*, the stage was transformed into a desert onto which the boys crash-landed through the forest canopy.

The magic of the space is the way in which the London sky casts a different natural light onto the action over the course of an evening. The opening act might embark in full natural sunlight, while the second will play out against a sunset of reds and yellows, fireflies dancing among the audience. Theatre has always thrived on its 'live'ness – the potential for the unknown and the collective sense that the audience might see something unique heightens the experience. But at this theatre even the actors are subject to the unpredictable – the weather – and the charge is tangible. The stage manager is in regular contact with the Met Office, as a performance can be paused, delayed or even hurried to factor in the approach of a storm. However, it's only the performers' safety that concerns the management; the seats are uncovered, but the shows have been known to go on through torrential rain. It is a truly organic and spontaneous experience, and, consequently, the relationship between audience and actor is more electric than ever.

An evening stroll through Little Venice (apparently given its name by the poet Robert Browning) with its picturesque waterways lined with canal boats and watering holes, leads conveniently to the **Canal Café Theatre**. Downstairs, fruit beers are the tipple of choice for regulars and upstairs, if the appetite for live entertainment still burns strong, NewsRevue, London's longest-running comic outing (it started in 1979), awaits.

AN ANIMAL MICROCOSM OF LONDON

The London Zoo is an animal microcosm of London, and even the lions, as a rule, behave as if they had been born in South Kensington.

Leonard Woolf

· ·

If Leonard Woolf was suggesting that the animals of London Zoo, 15,000 species in total, behaved with a decorum that set them apart from other animals, perhaps he wasn't privy, on his visits, to the male Egyptian tortoise, particularly vocal (for a tortoise) when mating, or bonobo chimps, who use sex in greeting and fighting rituals. The males are even known to enjoy a spot of 'penis fencing', whatever that entails.

London Zoo might be the world's oldest scientific zoo but it is always at the forefront in terms of its animal collection and exhibition – in 2005 the zoo even ran an exhibit which put eight humans on display for four days. Throughout the summer, Zoo Lates sees a 'raviary' atmosphere descend on the various enclosures, with cabaret, jazz, samba, comedy and even a silent disco on offer.

FROM PUBLIC HOUSES
TO MUSIC HALLS

Wapping

Wapping's greatest attraction is arguably the brooding foreshore of the River Thames itself, its wide and mysterious expanse lapping up against the foundations of some of Britain's oldest public houses. The **Prospect of Whitby** claims to be the oldest Thames-side pub in existence – it dates from 1543 – and in the seventeenth century built a reputation as a meeting place for smugglers and villains, hence the replica of the old Execution Dock gibbet that hangs menacingly over the water. This stretch of the river is tidal, and a number of algae-covered stone stairways (such as the Pelican Stairs near the Prospect of Whitby) dot the shoreline, the locations of which were a crucial part of a waterman's apprenticeship, for picking up and dropping off passengers – the predecessor to our London black cabbies' 'Knowledge'. Now, at low tide, amateur archaeologists and treasure hunters use them to trawl the beach for ancient pottery shards and other fragments of history.

The nearby **Wapping Project** is one of London's most original venues. Where Wapping Hydraulic Power Station once converted steam into power, the 1970s saw its conversion into a striking restaurant-cum-exhibition-and-performance space. The industrial integrity of the backdrop – the boiler and filter houses have been stripped back to their original 1890 form – has inspired countless sculptors and site-specific performances. The downstairs gallery focuses on photography, film and video with a well-curated programme of talks and events, but the restaurant itself lays equal claim to the venue's fine reputation, with

· ·

its in-house butchery for carnivores and carefully selected produce for veggies. It even manages to mix an element of performance into the dining experience with its plinth – a raised platform with eight tables where diners can observe everyone else, while everyone else observes them. There is an irrepressible sense of the area's true past when eating surrounded by the Victorian machinery that once hummed and whirred as it lit up Wapping's streets and homes. And continuing with the whole 'using spaces in unusual ways' theme, the **Wapping Project Bookshop** (see **Reading by the Fire**, overleaf) is in a tiny greenhouse adjacent to the main building.

A ten-minute walk towards Tower Hill finds a performance space that has had its fair share of survival scares over the years, but has emerged unscathed and more radiant than ever. **Wilton's Music Hall**, the world's oldest surviving grand music hall, might be the opposite of the grandeur traditionally associated with music halls, but boasts an undisputed charm and romance that Ben Stiller's Zoolander might have described as 'derelicte'. Standing in the elaborate gilt balconies and gazing down at the pillar-strewn auditorium, you can almost imagine the likes of Champagne Charlie performing to late-night audiences – along with a

performance of the first ever cancan, if the urban myths can be trusted (promptly banned immediately afterwards). Back then, a 'sun-burner' chandelier with 300 gas jets and 27,000 cut crystals adorned the ceiling; visible charring to the rafters is the only evidence remaining today.

During the war, it was the bombing of the London docks that threatened its destruction; in the '60s, it was the slum clearance and demolition plans, in 2004, a takeover by Weatherspoons, and in 2011, a rejected bid by the Lottery Fund for repair funds. But the fact that this theatre has attracted the support of stars ranging from Laurence Olivier to Liza Minnelli, from Peter Sellars to David Suchet, speaks for itself and the hall now plays host to the most eclectic programming, from 'Blitz' propaganda film nights to immersive adaptations of *The Great Gatsby*.

Back in its heyday, the Mahogany Bar was more famous across the globe for visiting sailors than St Paul's Cathedral; today, the mahogany fittings have gone but the spirit remains. The ping-pong table in the Green Room is a great accompaniment to a post-performance beer.

READING BY THE FIRE

Surrounded by tumbledown bamboo and clovers, the **Wapping Project Bookshop** is a place of magic all year round. A tiny greenhouse in the corner of the Wapping Project garden displays a selection of beautiful books, from special collector's editions to international magazines, in metal mesh cages alongside terracotta pots filled with cabbage and heather. The concept, architecturally, is that, against the backdrop of metal, glass, timber and cold white light, the books are left to glow and speak for themselves. In winter an antique wood-burning stove transports cosy readers far away from the industrial surroundings, but in summer, the bookshop throws open its glass doors and spills into the garden, with

deckchairs scattered about invitingly.

The bookshop was the brainchild of the Wapping Project's director, Jules Wright, who remembers 'living in my books' as a child. In a nod to a 'shop' she ran as a child in a disused henhouse, where she sold jars of soapy water to herself, imagining who she would be, her adult creation is a 'tiny glass bookshop with a coal fire … where everyone can browse and imagine who they might become, while others watch them through the glass and imagine who they are'.

Every Thursday night sees an event where an author, poet or designer talks about their work to an intimate audience under the starry Wapping sky.

FROM BROCKWELL PARK TO THE BRIXTON ACADEMY

· ·

Brixton

Before entering the intoxicating, bustling heart of Brixton, a moment's peace can be found hidden within the secret old English walled garden in **Brockwell Park**. A former kitchen garden for old Brockwell Hall, the rose beds still mix with herbaceous bedding in homage to their history. Volunteers from the local community have diligently converted a formerly derelict and fly-tipped site into two large greenhouses, complete with dye plant area, orchard and bee hives; traditional local produce is on sale alongside the more unusual bottle gourds, rice and ginger. But it's the park's lido, housed in a beautiful art deco Grade II-listed building, which attracts swimmers and BBQers alike, who head down to what is endearingly known as Brixton Beach on a sunny Friday evening.

Just across the other side of Brixton Hill is another landmark which has recently been at the heart of community renovation. The **Brixton Windmill** (see **Sailing Again**, p176), not to be mistaken for the popular music venue of the same name, is hidden away behind a terrace of tall Victorian houses, and with its new gleaming white sails, started grinding flour again in May 2011.

But for the most tangible immersion into the community's fiercely held identity, **Brixton Market** is second to none. Electric Avenue, the first market street to be lit by electricity, was the inspiration for Eddy Grant's 1982 hit single (we're gonna rock down to) 'Electric Avenue'. As the centre of London's Caribbean community, Brixton Market is a vibrant walk through stalls full of tropical fruit, jerk chicken, world music, wigs and the famous Brixton Snails (aka Giant African Land

Snails) – supposed to be eaten, mostly kept as pets.

But where a few years ago a number of lots stood empty, the traditional Brixton traders have now been joined by restaurants, coffee shops and boutiques in the covered Brixton Village. Now cafés offering curry goat and jerk chicken feel genuinely at home next to their 1950s-tea-dress-selling neighbours. Not only is it cheap and diverse, but the experience itself – squashed onto long tables in plain view of open, bustling kitchens – makes it worth the trip. Thanks to a council-generated 'free-rent' campaign, pop-ups sprung up left, right and centre. **Brixi**, one such curiosity-style shop, describes itself as 'like a museum but one where you can touch the exhibits'. Coeliacs can try a wheat- and gluten-free bun from **WAGfree**, **Honest Burgers** are tipped as the best inexpensive burger in London, and gelateria **LAB G** attracts regulars returning for its salted caramel ice cream.

The other highlight of SW9 is the grande dame of London's rock venues, **Brixton Academy**. Voted *NME*'s Venue of the Year twelve times since 1994, it has hosted the Sex Pistols reunion gigs, waved goodbye to the Smiths, and banned Leftfield after their decibel record-setting gig in 1996 started disintegrating the ceiling, resulting in showers of dust and plaster. Today, a more eclectic line-up sees the UK B-Boy championships and comedy nights give way to the Wu-Tang Clan reunion, Jack White and the Mystery Jets. The venue's interior sets it apart – the vast night-sky dome with its painted stars and planets, supported on either side of the proscenium by a Mediterranean townscape, makes it feel, for a few hours, like an outdoor concert in the balmy summertime. It is also one of the few venues where you have a decent view, wherever you stand, and at particularly hectic gigs, there is even a sweeping balcony upstairs with a long back row perfect for hiding away.

The nearby **Hootananny** offers a reggae and ska alternative to the Academy's line-up, while **The Effra**, a south London boozer on the outside, serves jerk chicken and rice washed down with Red Stripe to the unlikely strains of jazz. If your ears are still ringing, quieter alternatives are noodle bar **Fujiyama**, which endearingly offers 'a lot of Japanese all under one roof', and delicate French dining at **Upstairs**, with views to Victoria and beyond.

SAILING AGAIN

An original Regency building, Brixton Windmill was built in 1816 and run until 1934 by generations of the Ashby family, but once its sails came to a halt, it was left to deteriorate over many years, almost beyond recognition. When it was first built, it stood in open countryside with a cohort of other mills on the windy hills of Lambeth, but as the city began to grow up around it, the wind died away, forcing the Ashby family to install steam, then gas power, before giving up on the mill altogether. Even after it was given a Grade II listing, it continued to fall apart – many of the locals remember it as a permanent but unhappy landmark on the horizon – judged too dangerous for the public, a no-go area after dark – albeit a favourite playground for local children by day. The miller's cottage and all the other outbuildings around it were flattened one by one, but still the mill remained quietly resilient.

It wasn't until 2003 that the Friends of Windmill Gardens was formed, made up of actors, lawyers and other local volunteers, who, finding that the mill was surprisingly sound from a structural standpoint, set to work to restore it to its former glory. Not only does the provender mill, powered by electricity, work for days with no wind, but the windsails themselves now turn again, grinding flour from locally sourced wheat and barley.

FROM CULTURE
TO SCULPTURE

. . . .

King's Cross

And in the shadowless unclouded glare
Deep blue above us fades to whiteness
  where
A misty sea-line meets the wash of air.

  From John Betjeman's 'Cornish Cliffs'

In a sprawling area that was once synonymous with whorehouses and legendary all-night raves, the enormous goods yard behind King's Cross has undergone a radical facelift, clearing its 'badlands' reputation once and for all. The area has even been given a new postcode: NC1, and the developers are heralding it as the new cultural hub of central London, the proud host to fifty new arts and music venues. There are faint names on the brickwork – Coal Office, The Dockers Tavern, Imperial Gasworks – that evoke the days when this was the biggest transport interchange in the world. The finished site will house a linear park, named the Low Line (inspired by the high line equivalents in New York and Paris); Gasholder No. 8, a performance and entertainment space in a colossal disused gasholder guide frame; and Granary Square, one of the largest urban spaces of its kind in Europe, with a spectacular fountain of 1,120 jets.

One live venue can boast trailblazing credentials: **Kings Place** on York Way opened long before the developers pitched up. In 2008 it became the first public concert hall to be built in central London since the Barbican in 1982. The concert halls at Kings Place are quite unique: each sits on a bed of rubber springs to give it complete acoustic separation from the rest of the building – the only way to

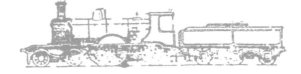

manage the noise of the hundreds of trains that pour in and out of King's Cross daily.

Be it folk on Fridays, jazz on Saturdays, or chamber music on Sundays, the musical line-up is both top-drawer and eclectic. But this is more than just a music venue: Off With Their Heads! boasts comedy club line-ups and the best Edinburgh shows – even the comedy giants occasionally take a break from their arena tours to play bespoke evenings. Words on Mondays features literary lecturing such as 'The Poetry of Bob Dylan', where poets, musicians, experts and Dylan junkies assemble to wax lyrical. One of the finest series is Not So Silent Movies, where bands and orchestras spontaneously jam a soundtrack to a classic silent film, all the more popular after the sudden upsurge of interest sparked by the Oscar-winning *The Artist*.

Live enlightenment continues just down the road at **The School of Life**, which appears to the outside eye as little more than an unassuming corner shop. But behind the façade lies a programme of lectures, classes, workshops and even sermons given by leading authors, artists, actors and academics, designed to grapple with every anxiety of (let's face it, middle-class) existence. From creativity to sex and intimacy workshops, from sermons on humility to talks on adultery, there is even an in-house bibliotherapist who 'prescribes' a bespoke reading list to her clients.

The area's major landmark is the new St Pancras railway station, which the poet Sir John Betjeman helped to save from demolition in the 1960s. Now, immortalised in bronze on the station concourse, a typically scruffy Betjeman looks up at the stunning arches of the shed, as he was wont to do, clutching his hat to his head and catching his breath in wonder. Dominating the concourse, however, is the nine-foot-tall kissing couple that stands beneath the railway clock (see **The Meeting Place**, overleaf), a more recent and controversial installation. The nearby **St Pancras Champagne Bar** is the longest bar in Europe and an unrivalled spot for people- and train-spotting. Blankets in wintertime keep out the cold, as does the Nebuchadnezzar of Taittinger, priced at £1,500 for those who can afford it.

The newly opened **St Pancras Hotel** houses the spectacular Gilbert Scott dining room and bar, its painted ceilings and bell chandeliers all designed by its namesake Sir George Gilbert Scott, where afternoon tea, cocktails or dinner are only a revolving door away.

For another space in keeping with the original King's Cross, **06 St Chad's Place** can be found down a back alley, where, 300 years ago, Londoners came from all corners of the capital to drink from St Chad's Well, whose water was rumoured to improve health. Now a Victorian warehouse has been tastefully reimagined in a Scandinavian style, with vast train-themed murals a homage to the area's heritage.

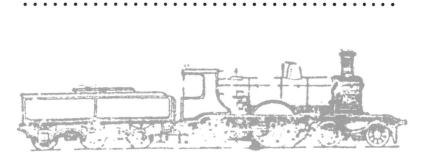

THE MEETING PLACE

When British artist Paul Day was commissioned to create a piece of art that would enhance and resonate within the scale and beauty of the Barlow shed of St Pancras station, he was told that it should reflect the romance that train travel used to have, and that it should be accessible, democratic and easily appreciated by the mass of people that go through the station on a daily basis.

Inspired by the opening scene of the Richard Curtis film *Love, Actually*, where a plethora of couples suddenly come together in a series of simultaneous reunions, Day's motivation was that an embracing couple under a clock is a universally recognised symbol of travel – with the clock becoming a moon at night. It was important to him that the silhouette of the sculpture, which he modelled on himself and his wife, resonated instantly from the other end of the station. The relief of getting together again after being apart comes from the sense that 'all separation involves a suspended moment when one wonders, "Is this forever?"'

 # SOHO NIGHTS

A round-up of the best live music venues in Soho.

12 Bar Club

26 Denmark Street, WC2H 8NN

This is a truly tiny live music venue but it has punched considerably above its weight over the years, with the Libertines, Seasick Steve and Martha Wainwright all past crooners taking to its rouge-swamped stage.

100 Club

100 Oxford Street, W1D 1LL

Another small gig venue in central London which gained its legendary status in the late 1970s through the punk movement, with the Clash and the Sex Pistols both regulars. These days, it often has 'secret' last-minute concerts with big names, as well as regular swing nights, with lessons before the party starts.

Ray's Jazz at Foyles

· ·

113–119 Charing Cross Road, WC2H 0EB

Read each other excerpts from your favourite books or just sit and listen to the free concerts and events that take place on the first floor of this venerable West End bookshop, including improvised sets of freeform jazz.

Madame JoJos

· ·

8–10 Brewer Street, W1F 0SE

Madame JoJo's became a celebrated cabaret venue in the 1970s and '80s, with legendary drag artistes performing there. With the recent resurgence of burlesque and variety acts, it continues to host some of the world's best live acts and guarantees an ever-so-naughty night out.

Floridita

· ·

100 Wardour Street, W1F 0TN

Against the backdrop of an iconic restaurant and bar which serves the infamous Floridita cocktail with an impressive mix of rums, the live programme aims to combine the old-world glamour and decadence of a bygone era, namely the 1930s of the original El Floridita.

Ain't Nothing But Blues Bar

· ·

20 Kingly Street, W1B 5PZ

Tucked down a side street lies this little corner of the American Deep South; an authentic slice of Americana: sticky dark wood, guitars hanging from the low ceiling and walls adorned with posters of Muddy Waters. If you're lucky, you'll grab one of the six tables around the band.

The Borderline

. . . .

Orange Yard, Manette Street, W1D 4JB

Despite its rather unprepossessing
entrance off a scrappy yard, and its
faux-saloon decor, the Borderline is
regarded as a Soho musical institution.
The basement venue has featured
most musical genres from Britpop to
grunge and alternative folk and all
points in between, but is best known
for its focus on country, folk, blues and
Americana acts.

The Crobar

. . . .

17 Manette Street, W1D 4AS

Known best as a late-night dive bar
with lots of attitude, a jukebox and
an extensive range of bourbons, the
Crobar also stages the odd gig and
comedy event. It's impossible to have
a bad night out at this place.

Terrace Bar at the Montague Hotel

. . . .

15 Montague Street, WC1B 5BJ

A classy old-school drinking den
with lovely leather armchairs to sink
into and listen to the live music, with
one of their excellent classic cocktails
in hand.

FROM DINOSAURS
TO LEATHER JACKETS

· ·

Crystal Palace

As you pull into Crystal Palace overground station, a glance through the foliage gives you a sneak preview of the prehistoric dinosauria that inhabits **Crystal Palace Gardens**. Guarding the secrets to these stony giants and the other ruins scattered throughout these sprawling plains are a gaggle of local experts at the modest but charming **Crystal Palace Museum** which is on your left as you head into the park. A quick wander through the trail of black-and-white photos, housed in the old engineering school where television's inventor John Logie Baird worked, brings the park's glory days to life, chronicling the great history of Joseph Paxton's once-spectacular building before the great fire of 1936 left most of it razed to the ground.

The underpopulated zoo (mainly goats and farm animals) faces the National Sports Centre stadium across the trail down to Dinosaur Court, the extraordinary nineteenth-century collection of 'lifesize' monsters that swim, stride and climb their way about the trees and ponds of the Lower Lake (see **Walking with Dinosaurs**, p192).

Tall trees reach for each other over the park's main avenue, a central axis that was built to connect the park's main Penge entrance to the staircases of the Palace itself. In the summer, the beech trees are in full foliage, making the maze (dating back to 1872) worth a quick detour en route to the northwest of the park, where the Palace once stood. Though no longer home to weekly Sunday concerts from the London Philharmonic or the likes of Bob Marley, who played there in the early 1980s, the Concert Bowl still holds gigs from time to time,

including, most recently, the South London Calling festival.

The northernmost corner of the park houses the ruins of the Aquarium, a marine home that, when built in 1871, was the largest of its kind in the world. Tanks of saltwater were brought by train from the sea in Brighton to fill the sixty fishtanks. It proved a huge success until the 1890s, when monkeys became the new fish and the tanks were converted into menageries. The aquarium survived the southward-blowing fire which destroyed the Palace, but collapsed when the North Tower was dynamited a few years later – rumour has it so that the Luftwaffe wouldn't use it as a landmark to guide them into central London.

A trip down Old Cople Lane, a name derived from the Old French word meaning 'couple', heralds the remains of the Palace itself. Sweeping terraces are guarded by a handful of sphinx (all cast from the same original in the Louvre) and a solitary sultan looking mournfully towards the east.

The gardens' colonialist memorials give way to a thriving community of boutique stores and cafés along Church Road, celebrated in local comedian Daniel Kitson's theatre monologue *66a Church Road*. The road was once home to Angela Carter's Magic Toyshop (now, rather unmagically, an accounting firm). The jewel in the crown is **Bambino**, a treasure trove of vintage leather jackets (as worn by Kate Moss and photographed in store by Mario Testino in 2008), mannequins sporting biker goggles or plastic leashes, antique comic books, furniture from every decade, and a 'to-go' coffee bar.

Amid the abundance of local vintage and antiques shops, the one not to miss is the **Antiques Warehouse**, on Jasper Road, a warren of interconnecting rooms of furniture spread over four floors, selling everything from 1950s anglepoise desk lamps and gilded mirrors in the basement, to mahogany dining tables upstairs. On the same corner, the **Exhibition Rooms** restaurant does down-to-earth food really well and its interior was inspired by the design of the former Crystal Palace.

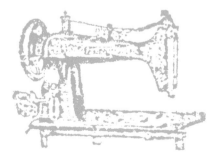

WALKING WITH DINOSAURS

For over 150 years, the grounds of the Crystal Palace have been the playing fields of fifteen apparently life-sized dinosaur sculptures, the very first in the world, predating Darwin's *The Origin of Species* by six years and created only a decade after the earliest discovery of dinosaur remains in Britain.

Sculptor Benjamin Waterhouse Hawkins and celebrated naturalist Richard Owen were commissioned to create these models at the time that the Crystal Palace was uprooted from Hyde Park to Sydenham Hill, following the closure of the Great Exhibition (for which the Palace itself was created). Owen and Hawkins launched the models with an extravagant party hosted in the belly of one of the iguanodons on New Year's Eve, 1853.

The models were laid out across three islands, which represented the different geologic eras, and the 'tidal' lake, in which the semi-aquatic beasts lay, rose and fell to expose different parts of the dinosaurs, attempting to breathe a sense of life into the creatures.

They are, for the most part, now considered anatomically inaccurate – the seal-like ichthyosaurus has beached itself fatally; the iguanodon's thumb-spike has migrated northwards to the crest of his nose; and the iconic megalosaurus skulks about on all fours rather than on two legs.

Nevertheless, these scientific quibbles fail to detract from the childlike wonder at the first sight of a scaly outstretched neck and head reaching through the tree branches towards you.

FROM EEL PIE ISLAND TO STRAWBERRY HILL

· ·

Twickenham

Unto the Eel-Pie Island at Twickenham: there to make merry upon a cold collation, bottled beer, shrub, and shrimps, and to dance in the open air to the music of a locomotive band.

Charles Dickens, *Nicholas Nickleby*

A rainbow-shaped footbridge spans the River Thames, separating the residents of Eel Pie Island from Twickenham embankment and the rest of the world. No motor vehicles are allowed to break the peace of this shipyard and artists' commune and the only way in is via this bridge or by boat. A single lane leads past the island's noticeboard, on which is pinned a note reading: 'Wanted. Woman to cook and clean fish, dig worms and make love. Must have good boat and motor. Please include photo of boat and motor.' Each house is unique, hidden behind an array of façades and foliages, each hand-painted sign hinting at the character and history of the artist within. The residents are famously private and wary of outsiders and there is no shortage of 'Keep Out' signs – one tacked to a tree reads, 'Wrong Day. Go Back'.

A short way past the colourful tiled front steps of the infamous Love Shack (see **Love Shack**, p200) are a set of large blue metal gates, the gateway to the **Eel Pie Island art studios**. These are closed to the public with the exception of two weekends in the year, one in June and one in December – the precise times are available on the island's website. The smell of solder and boat oil permeates the air in the vast boatyard on the other

side of the gates, which gives way to a sprawling jungle of wooden studios, mini sculpture parks and pottery shards. A maze of pathways between boat hulls leads visitors past a giant shark's head consuming a human bust, and a skeleton that peers ominously out from inside a suspended birdcage. In the carved porthole of an old boat that doubles as a workshop, a little toy figurine battles his way past mini ferns. Every studio is proudly adorned with names of the artists who carve or sculpt or paint inside, including potter Judith Rowe (her signature long-legged birds adorning her beautiful jugs and plates), and Rosa Diaz, one of the more famous residents, whose front garden is festooned with naked Barbie dolls, liberated from Mattel many years ago. People now leave dolls on her lawn – a kind of orphanage for lost toys.

The studios are a melting pot of creativity and the sense of artistic heritage is palpable. But it is for music and revelry that the island is truly renowned. As early as the Tudor period, Henry VIII is said to have enjoyed filling his stomach with eel pies on his way down the river from Hampton Court to his various mistresses and, years later, Charles Dickens too enjoyed a beer at the Eel Pie Hotel. It was this establishment that became a tea-dance venue in the 1920s and then the Mecca for traditional jazz in the late 1950s. The old hotel had a sprung dance floor which acted like a trampoline, bouncing the inebriated groupies up and down as they danced to the likes of Cyril Davies and Memphis Slim. Back then the only way onto the island was by punt, with a fierce old lady guarding the tollbooth entrance at a rate of tuppence per head.

In the 1960s, 'Eelpiland' became the epicentre of the British rhythm and blues movement and hundreds of revellers would descend to drink, party and dance every weekend. On 24 April 1963, the Rolling Stones played the island for the first time, paving the way for The Who, Eric Clapton, Jeff Beck, David Bowie (then David Jones) and Pink Floyd. To get on and off the island, one needed an 'Eelpiland passport', which read, 'We request and require in the name of His Excellency Prince Pan all those whom it may concern to give the Bearer of this Passport ... any assistance he/she may require in his/her lawful business of Jiving and generally Cutting a Rug.' Rod Stewart, then singing with

Long John Baldry, would strut about, wearing a three piece suit, his hair bouffant, constantly trying to 'pull a bit of crumpet'.

The club closed in 1967 after the hotel's condition deteriorated, briefly re-opening as the prog-happy Colonel Barefoot's Rock Garden, attracting, according to Chris Faiers' Eel Pie Dharma, '200 dossers, hippies, runaway school kids, drug dealers, petty thieves, heroin addicts, artists, poets, bikers, American hippy tourists, au pair girls and Zen philosophers'. The hotel itself was destroyed in a fire in 1971, heralding the end of its glory days.

Of the thirty dwellings on Eel Pie Island, **Ripple** is a charming self-catering riverside chalet brought all the way from the Transylvanian forests, available for short-term lets. Back on the mainland the nearby Church Street hosts a collection of cafés, bars and restaurants, which go Continental during the summer with al fresco dining on Thursday, Friday and Saturday evenings. An all-weather alternative is the newly renovated pub **The Fox**, which even has bacon sandwiches on the menu.

An equally curious detour is **Strawberry Hill House**, a ten-minute walk from Church Street. The brainchild of Horace Walpole in the eighteenth century, Strawberry Hill is Britain's finest example of Georgian Gothic revival architecture. Waking from a dream one night, Walpole imagined he saw a giant armoured fist on the staircase, which became the inspiration for the first Gothic novel, *The Castle of Otranto*. Printed on the first private printing press in the country at Strawberry Hill, it was in turn the inspiration for Mary Shelley's *Frankenstein*. A tour of Strawberry Hill House is a theatrical experience, just as Walpole intended, the plain white exterior and grey stone staircase giving way to the sumptuous state apartment – a burst of crimson and gold.

LOVE SHACK

One of the most infamous couples of Eel Pie Island are artists Simon and Sheba Cassini, who were determined to call their home 'Love Shack' after the famous hit by '80s pop band the B-52s, itself inspired by the island.

The Cassinis battled for eight months with Richmond Council, which was convinced that the change of name would prove confusing to any emergency services needing to find the house. The council's official advice was to replace the word 'shack' with any of the following: 'apartment, building, centre, court, heights, house, lodge, mansions, point, studio, tower or villa'. When a neighbour called the fire brigade, mistaking a garden barbeque for an actual fire, three fire engines successfully found the shack, proving the council's fears unfounded.

The Cassinis' Love Shack went on to win in an ITV show, *May The Best House Win*.

FROM LAUDERDALE TO LAUDANUM

. . . .

Highgate Cemetery

Far too neat. These people seem to have died with white gloves on.

Gustave Flaubert,
on Highgate Cemetery

It may formerly have been the private digs of London's Lord Mayor (back in the sixteenth century) but lunch at **Lauderdale House** is unpretentious and wholesome, set against the backdrop of **Waterlow Park**, bequeathed to the public as a 'garden for the gardenless' in 1889. Andrew Marvell has left his mark on the terrace sundial with the words 'One is nearer to God in a garden than anywhere else on earth'. This hidden oasis is often dotted, but never crowded, with lovers picnicking beneath the Strawberry Tree (whose fruit does not taste like strawberries, but instead is rather insipid and not

to everyone's taste, though it can be used for post-partum contraception, apparently).

The park is bordered on two sides by the world-renowned **Highgate Cemetery**, which pays morbid homage to romance and memory. The cemetery is one of a collection known as the 'Magnificent Seven', built in Victorian times to alleviate overcrowding in the inner-city parish grounds. Attitudes to mourning have changed since the cemetery's inception in 1939 – back then, the appropriate mourning period for women mourning their men was two years; for the widower, a mere six months.

The West Cemetery feels straight out of a Brothers Grimm fairy tale, with its spectacular obelisks, gothic catacombs and ivy-covered

· ·

mausoleums scattered over 17 acres of overgrown woodland. It can only be seen on an official tour and Audrey Niffenegger, author of *The Time Traveller's Wife*, became so preoccupied with the place that she became a tour guide to research her second novel (on the strict proviso that the book avoid all references to sex in the cemetery). The cemetery is the resting place of, among others, Charles Cruft, who created the famous dog show to market his dog-biscuit enterprise (but who was ironically a cat-lover); Alexander Litvinenko, whose lead coffin is a necessary precaution against radioactivity; and the Rossetti family (see **Love Preserved**, overleaf). World-champion pugilist Thomas Sayers' grave is guarded by his large bloodhound named Lion, who reportedly was closer to Tom than his own wife and took her place as chief mourner in the funeral cortège. Back in the days of bare-knuckle fighting, Tom's fight with American fighter John Camel Heenan was considered boxing's first world championship. After five rounds, Sayers had dislocated and

broken his right arm, but, with his left, managed to close Heenan's eyes – it was a blind man fighting a one-armed man. The fight went on for forty-two rounds, before the ring was charged by onlookers, descending into chaos, and the fight declared a draw.

The East Cemetery can be seen unaccompanied, and holds the main attraction: the tomb of Karl Marx, now a listed monument. But by no means does he hold court alone; writer George Eliot is reunited with her true identity (Mary Ann Evans), while artist Peter Caulfield's gravestone is simply four giant stone letters spelling DEAD. Vigilance is key (an excuse for keeping close together); the cemetery became famous in the 1960s and '70s for sightings of the Highgate Vampire, 'a tall black figure with a deathly white face', perhaps a descendant of Bram Stoker's Lucy Westenra, buried and then reborn in the cemetery.

Karl Marx's favourite pub **The Flask**, with its labyrinth of candlelit tunnels and snug corners, provides a gothically romantic setting for dinner.

LOVE PRESERVED

Nestled deep into the West Cemetery is a collection of gravestones all belonging to the relations of the great pre-Raphaelite painter and poet Dante Gabriel Rossetti, although not the poet himself. One of the graves belongs to Elizabeth Siddal, the muse and model for many iconic paintings, including most of Rossetti's earliest paintings and Millais' *Ophelia*. For the latter, when one of the lamps burning beneath the bath went out, the bathwater in which she posed became icy cold, but Millais was so engrossed that he failed to notice and Siddal contracted pneumonia.

Infatuated with her, Rossetti became engaged to Siddal, but he repeatedly called off the wedding at the last minute, leaving her in an increased state of stress and depression. She developed an addiction to laudanum, on which she overdosed shortly after her first child was stillborn. However, suicide was still illegal – in fact, 1882, some twenty years later, was the final date recorded on which suicides were buried at crossroads with a stake driven through the heart. Rossetti had the suicide note destroyed to allow Siddal a Christian burial, and intertwined a collection of his poems within her long red locks of hair. By this time he himself was an addict and had begun to go blind. Seven years later, convinced that he needed the poems to restore his failing career, he arranged for Siddal's body to be exhumed. Her corpse was said to be perfectly preserved, her beauty as radiant as ever, and her hair had continued to grow and now filled the coffin. The poems were not a success (due to their erotic nature) and Rossetti was haunted by what he had done for the rest of his life.

FROM THE HACKNEY PEARL
TO THE OLYMPIC PARK

. . . .

Hackney Wick

'The Wick' is the new Dalston, the current domicile of choice for 'penniless' artists, rippling eastwards in a bid to stay ahead of London's gentrification. That said, since the likes of the controversial Chapman brothers moved in (regularly spotted in the local greasy spoon), it has become known by some as 'Hackney Chic' (which doesn't even rhyme).

It is an area in a constant state of flux; there is a good chance that any pop-up street market or gallery mentioned here may be there one day, gone the next – the clue's in the name. But in its place will be a 'secret' supperclub or deli-café-flea market-record store. That's the very charm of the place – it's a moveable feast. And beneath the façade of crumbling warehouses and giant graffiti murals is a fiercely loyal community and the highest concentration of artists' studios in the world. Some of London's most important artists live and work in the area, including Michael Landy, Phyllida Barlow and Gary Webb.

A great time to visit is the annual Hackney Wicked art festival at the end of July, but most days of the year feature something strange but wonderful. Take **Scrap Club**, one of London's weirdest nights out, recently featured in a car park in Hackney Wick, where customers were invited to take their pick of sledgehammers, crowbars, bats and pipes and to destroy anything from televisions to fridges in a surreal evening of revenge on the machine; or **Films on Fridges**, a temporary cinema projected onto a mountain of discarded fridges and freezers.

The **Hackney Pearl** is a good brunch spot to plot your local adventure, over its self-proclaimed best Bloody Marys in London. There is an array of comfy and designer (non-comfy) chairs, scattered-about Formica tables and bookshelves lined with old copies of *National Geographic*. Most customers seem to arrive on Dutch bicycles sporting moustaches and vintage spectacles. But don't let that put you off …

Every month the local sartorialists and fashionistas spread yesterday's (surprisingly decent) wardrobes across the streets and stalls in the vintage **Flea Market**. If the collection of onesies and pointy shoes gets too much, then the more mainstream (but still achingly fashionable) **Broadway Market** is only a canal walk away.

The **Yard Theatre**, on Queen's Yard, is a triumph of pop-up turned permanent, a 110-seat performance space aimed at a perceived lack of opportunity for young directors to show new and challenging work. Its pink ply-board rake is made up from materials discarded by Olympic developers in what would appear an innovative use of resources. And yet the locals, on first arrival, made their feelings on any Games-related arts developments clear by ripping

down its signs and spraying 'Olympic Gentrification Area' on a wall outside (see **Olympic Invasion**, opposite) – clearly, not all art is welcome. Across the courtyard is **Elevator Gallery**, housed in a former chocolate factory, one of the many galleries to be priced out of the Shoreditch renaissance.

The **Stour Space** houses an exhibition space, the monthly Designers' Market and the superb **Counter Café** split over two levels, which has great views of the Olympic Park and Stadium, home-made pies and blue retro flip-up theatre seats. The Stour Space describes itself as 'A socially minded organisation offering exhibition, performance and studio space for the development of creative enterprises' (which, on reflection, sounds like the majority of Hackney Wick establishments). But before any cynicism creeps in, it's worth remembering that Hackney Wick's creative past stretches back to the Victorian era, when it was a hotbed of innovation: the diode, plastic, the word 'petrol', dry cleaning and the toilet roll were all invented in Hackney. Most recently, Sugru, a miracle silicon product that is supposedly able to fix or mend anything, has been developed there.

And so Hackney Wick continues to innovate, morph and surprise. Poking around disused warehouses, scrap yards and former factories might not be up everyone's street, but not knowing what you might stumble upon around the next corner is part of Hackney Wick's irresistible, idiosyncratic charm.

The development of the Olympic Park has been the subject of much dispute, no more so than for the local businesses and artists originally attracted to the area by its low rent and large warehouse spaces. One of the godfathers of local trade is **H. Forman & Son**, arguably the finest salmon smokehouse in the world, aptly located on Hackney Wick's Fish Island.

Forman & Son has seen four generations of salmon smokers supply fish to celebrity chefs including Gordon Ramsey and Marcus Wareing, and British institutions ranging from the House of Lords to Zuma. Lance Forman, the current manager, is passionate about the localness of the trade – contrary to most people's assumption that smoking hails from Scotland, it is an East End business started by Ashkenazi Jews from Eastern Europe who capitalised on the freshness of the salmon from Billingsgate market.

When the plans for the Olympic Stadium were finalised, Formans was served a relocation order with the assurance that no business would be 'worse off'. After fierce court battles, the Olympic powers agreed to rebuild the factory on a site overlooking the Stadium, with a restaurant and a gallery that exhibits work by local artists.

And while many continue to object to the disruptive impact of the games, others have taken a more off beat approach: artist Hilary Powell created her 'Olympic Spirit', a home brew made from berries picked on the Olympic site before the diggers arrived.

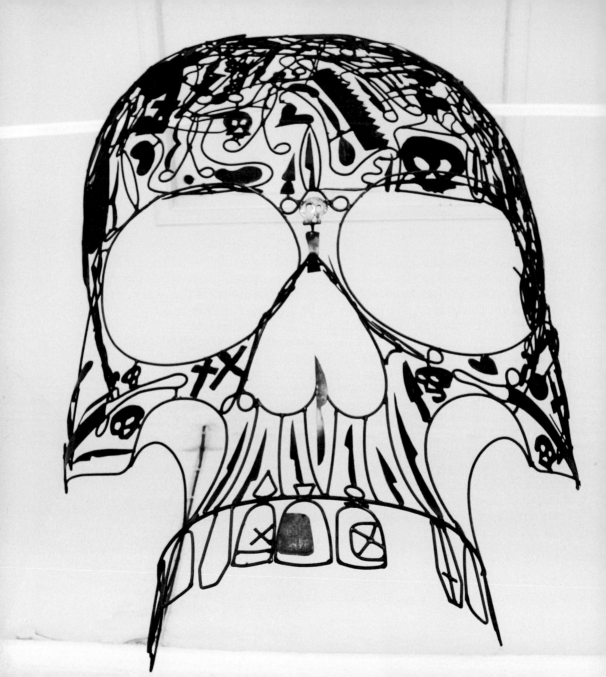

WEIRD & WONDERFUL

A selection of the curious and curiouser
places to take your date in the capital.

The London Buddhist Centre

51 Roman Road, E2 0HU

You can discover your inner chakras
together at one of their drop-in
lunchtime meditation classes, or
longer courses at the weekend.

The Chin Chin Laboratorists

49–50 Camden Lock Place, NW1 8AF

'Laboratorist' husband-and-wife team
Ahrash and Nyisha use liquid nitrogen
to make ice cream at 'Europe's first
liquid nitrogen ice cream parlour'.

The Victoria and Albert Museum

. . . .

Cromwell Road, SW7 2RL

One of the lesser-known highlights of the V&A is going for a paddle at the V&A's John Madejski Garden. Set in the V&A's Italianate courtyard, the garden features at its centre a stone-paved oval, surrounded by water jets, and is either filled with water as a paddling pool, or drained for displays.

The Berkeley Hotel

. . . .

Wilton Place, SW1X 7RL

The Berkeley does afternoon tea for the style-conscious with its impeccably served Prêt-à-Portea. Cakes and pastries are designed to resemble the latest catwalk collections from a range of designers and changes with the season (naturally).

The International Magic Shop

. . . .

89 Clerkenwell Road, EC1R 5BX

You can take a course on everything from floating tables to tricks for the amateur, or simply browse their excellent collection of props, books and DVDs for magicians from the aspiring to the expert.

The Last Tuesday Society and Viktor Wynd's Little Shop of Horrors

. . . .

11 Mare Street, E8 4RP

Tucked away from the traffic of Hackney's Mare Street, this basement shop, designed in the style of a seventeenth-century *Wunderkabinett*, sells all manner of 'natural and human curiosities', from nineteenth-century shrunken heads to stuffed bats and narwhal tusks.

Liberation

49 Shelton Street, WC2H 9HE

If you're into a bit of old-school bedroom antics, this antique fetish shop in Covent Garden offers opportunities for role play with a Victorian bridle and spurs, ivory dildos or, for the really intrepid, a World War I operating table with original straps.

Dawn Chorus Walk

Hampstead Heath

Pad noiselessly into the Hampstead woods at four in the morning, the rest of your group invisible in the darkness. As the sun rises, the trees are suddenly filled with the rising cacophony of waking robins, blackbirds and crows. Summer months only.

Late-night Basketball at Midnight Madness

Various locations

Originally set up to combat gun crime, this late-night competition is now the largest open-participation basketball tournament in the country, watched by thousands of spectators. The likes of Michael Jordan and Busta Rhymes have got involved with the programme.

Old Operating Theatre Museum

9 St Thomas Street, SE1 9RY

Nestled within the herb garret of St Thomas' Church in Southwark, this museum is the oldest surviving operating theatre in Europe, on the grounds of the old St Thomas' Hospital. When it opened, hordes of students would pour into the theatre to watch operations.

FROM TOWERING MONUMENTS TO ANCIENT RUINS

· ·

The City of London

Heads down and brows furrowed, London's city slickers scurry from the foyer of one glass-fronted skyscraper to another. Behind all this commerce, it's hard to believe that London's financial centre, the Square Mile, has the highest concentration of historical buildings of anywhere in London. From the ruins of ancient Roman Londinium through to the stomping ground for Dickens' most infamous characters, the churches, alleyways and monuments of the City are best explored during the week: when the stock markets stop trading, so do all the other markets, local shops and even churches, and the City becomes a ghost town.

The starting point of this City stroll stands proudly at 202 feet tall: the **Monument**, marking the point where the Great Fire of 1666 first blazed and commemorating the rebuilding of the City in its wake. A few quid and 311 steep steps bring you out in front of a sculpted explosion of gold flames and one of the best panoramic views of London there is. Back on ground level, just up Philpot Lane you'll find **Leadenhall Market** – London's most beautiful Victorian market, with its ornate gabled glass roofs designed by Horace Jones (who also designed nearby Smithfield Market). The market has been a prime location for film shoots – including *Harry Potter* – not surprising, given how the period feel has been immaculately preserved: even the mobile phone shops and hairdressers have the original trade names printed on their ye olde façades.

At 54–55 Cornhill, three terracotta devil statues perch upon a Victorian office block, behind which lies a dark

story of revenge. Before construction started on the site, the vicar of next-door St Peter upon Cornhill noticed that the plans encroached marginally onto the church's property. He complained so vociferously that the architect was forced to change his plans; but the architect had the last laugh: his new design had three grotesques overlook the church, scorning those who entered. Off Cornhill, where in *A Christmas Carol* Bob Cratchit 'went down a slide … twenty times in honour of its being Christmas-eve', a sharp turn into Ball Court plunges you away from the noise of the main road and into another world. The gloomy maze of alleyways isn't really about taking you anywhere in particular except to imagine (as Dickens did) Ebeneezer Scrooge's counting house and the sound of Scrooge's neighbours 'stamping their feet upon the pavement stones'. Tucked away in these back streets you will also find the **Jamaica Wine House**, on the site of London's first ever coffee house, which Samuel Pepys himself frequented.

But while Scrooge was a product of Dickens' imagination, the real-life object of his affections lived just around the corner. Maria Beadnell, of Lombard Street, spent four years toying with the young reporter thirteen months her junior. Her parents never considered him an appropriate suitor and Maria was sent away to finishing school. When she came back to the City, she had gone off him and he was left to wander Lombard Street in the early hours, lovesick and staring up at the house where she slept.

The Royal Exchange towers over the other side of Cornhill, recently restored to its nineteenth-century splendour, and filled with luxury shops selling cashmere, fur and fancy underwear. At the nearby **No. 1 Poultry**, one of London's oldest archeological artefacts, a wooden drain dated to AD 47, can be found beneath the hordes of noisy city slickers who flock to the fashionable rooftop **Coq d'Argent** restaurant to see the view and to be seen.

Round the corner, nestled in between modern office blocks, is the **Church of St Stephen Walbrook**, claimed in 1734 as the 'masterpiece of the celebrated Sir Christopher Wren' with no rival for taste or proportion in all of Italy. Inside it gets better – with the altar carved by another design genius,

Henry Moore. Initially Moore wasn't convinced by the request, due to his agnosticism, but the rector's response put him straight: 'Henry, I'm not asking you to take the service. I understand that you're a bit of a chiseller; just do your job!'

It's not only Moore's handiwork that has been dealt with flippantly; the nearby Roman **Temple of Mithras** (a virile young god) was front-page news in 1954 and even attracted Churchill's attention, when it was deemed to be in the way of a seven-storey office block. The developers, Legal & General, paid for it to be transplanted to a nearby car park. In 2012, it got in the way again, this time of Bloomberg LP, who are paying for it to be returned to its original location.

A wiggle along Cheapside past an unimpressive statue with a heartwarming story (see **The Naughty One**, overleaf), and up Old Jewry and Frederick's Place, is a cosy huddle of distinguished houses, with a distinguished former inhabitant. Years before he became Prime Minister, Benjamin Disraeli worked as a solicitor's clerk at Number 6. Back then, he was known for sporting a certain sartorial flair which marked him apart from his contemporaries, and a particularly prescient colleague once told him: 'You have too much genius for Frederick's Place, it will never do.'

From one illustrious leader to another, around the corner you will find **Guildhall,** the official seat of the Lord Mayor of London. The main square is an architectural hodge-podge from the towering spires of the Gothic grand entrance to the spiky crown-like turrets of the Modernist Guildhall Library – there is something eerie and intimidating about the juxtaposition of such imposing designs in one space. But it's much further underground that London's most distant past is on display: on the bottom level of the Guildhall Art Gallery are the remains of Londinium's Roman Amphitheatre, just as they were discovered when the gallery was built. Only the foundations of the gateway remain – but the sheer proximity to the 2,000-year-old brickwork, combined with the Guildhall's light projections designed to recreate the design of the structure, make for a surreal journey back in time.

Love Lane, frequented either by medieval prostitutes or just couples in love, depending on which historian you believe, leads in the direction of **Postman's Park**, best known for the profound Watts Memorial, in homage to those who have sacrificed their lives for others (see p37).

Two giants of sacred architecture compete for your final destination; heading south from Postman's Park, one of London's most iconic landmarks: **St Paul's Cathedral**. It may have the world's third-largest dome, but its greatest charm is the Whispering Gallery, where you can stand at different ends of the vast circle and whisper each other sweet nothings. To the north, **St Bartholomew the Great** is London's oldest parish church, and with its atmosphere of 'holy gloom' has featured in films including *Shakespeare in Love* and *Four Weddings and a Funeral*. One couple's dedication to each other is celebrated on a wall monument with the inscription:

Shee first deceased, hee for a little Tryd
To live without her, Liked it not and dyd.

THE NAUGHTY ONE

St Mary-le-Bow is essential to a number of folklorish tales; tradition dictates that a true Cockney must be born within earshot of its bells and indeed it was those very bells that turned Dick Whittington back from Highgate to stay in London to become Lord Mayor.

But perhaps the most fascinating story to emanate from the church features one of its parishioners, English adventurer John Smith, now immortalised in bronze in

the church square. Smith was captured by a group of Native American Indians as he set about settling the state of Virginia. On the verge of being beaten to death by several warriors, his fate was changed by the audacity of the chieftain's eight-year-old daughter, who took Smith's head in her arms and laid her own upon his to save him from death. The girl was none other than Pocahontas, or 'the naughty one'.

FROM THE 1690s
TO THE 1960s

· ·

Hampstead

One man can learn more in a journey by the Hampstead coach than another can by making the Grand Tour of Europe.

Samuel Johnson

Today, Hampstead may have an abundance of boutique clothing stores and organic delis, but behind its upmarket High Street lies a historic trail of buildings, a literary and architectural heritage that spans the last four centuries. Hampstead's houses have borne witness to the intimate lives of some of England's most iconic cultural figures, immortalised in the lyricism of Keats and Leigh Hunt and the sharp wit of John Mortimer and Kingsley Amis.

Fenton House, the oldest surviving Hampstead mansion, is a formal introduction to Hampstead's past, built in 1693 as an out-of-town merchant's residence. There are fine examples of needlework and Georgian furniture (if you like that sort of thing), but the more eccentric appeal lies in the regular concerts it stages using the extensive collection of eighteenth-century harpsichords, virginals and spinets. Summer concerts with picnics are staged among the rose and lavender gardens, and once a year on Apple Day (late September) visitors can taste the thirty different types of apple grown in the 300-year-old orchard. It may not be *The X Factor*, but the annual Battle of Baroque Bands, in early May, draws quite a crowd to vote for their favourite period piece.

The original reason for Hampstead's fashionable status was the chalybeate waters (water impregnated with iron) of Hampstead Wells, attracting residents and drawing visitors on account of its restorative powers. Although the Wells were destroyed in 1882, a solitary fountain still exists on Well Walk. Just around the corner is **Burgh House**, built in 1704 and a relic from those halcyon days. It was occupied by the physician who discovered the healing powers of the springs and later by the daughter of Rudyard Kipling. It now houses the Hampstead Museum, with a permanent exhibition on local artist John Constable.

Just down the hill is Keats Grove, home to the much-loved **Keats House** where poet John Keats lived from 1818 to 1820, before leaving for Italy to die alone. The house is a celebration of his life, his work and his death. Most of Keats' possessions were burnt in Italy when he died, which meant that his only surviving legacy consists of the few artefacts still displayed in the house, and of course his poetry. It was here that the tragic love affair which inspired some of the most romantic poems ever written had its brief existence (see **I Cannot Breathe Without You**, p232).

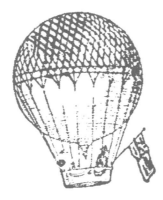

It's hard not to be moved by the tiny
room where Keats first coughed up
his 'life blood' and understood his fate.
But it's the gardens – each border
reflecting an aspect of his poetry:
Melancholy, Autumn and Nightingale –
where Keats dreamt up his most
famous poem, 'Ode to a Nightingale',
underneath a plum tree.

Away! away! for I will fly to thee,
      Not charioted by Bacchus and his pards,
But on the viewless wings of Poesy,
      Though the dull brain perplexes and retards:
Already with thee! tender is the night,
      And haply the Queen-Moon is on her throne,
            Cluster'd around by all her starry Fays;
                  But here there is no light,
      Save what from heaven is with the breezes blown
            Through verdurous glooms and winding mossy ways.

From John Keats 'Ode to a Nightingale'

Back towards the High Street and on
to the twentieth century at modernist
architect Erno Goldfinger's house
at **2 Willow Road**, built in 1939 and
unchanged since. It's a wonder of
modernist architecture built of
concrete and glass, with moveable
partitions and folding doors, spiral
staircases and detailed light switches,

all designed by Goldfinger. The subtle use of colour palettes, growing lighter and brighter as you climb, makes you feel like you're working your way towards the sky. But Hampstead resident Ian Fleming was not so enamoured by the design and promptly named his most iconic Bond villain after 2 Willow Road's creator.

As this journey through Hampstead's past loops back to the High Street and draws closer to the present day, Starbucks has a much older rival: one of London's oldest coffee shops, **The Coffee Cup**, which opened in 1953 and has counted Dudley Moore, Peter Cook, Sting, Sir Paul McCartney and Emma Thompson among its regulars. For dining, rustic French institution **Le Cellier du Midi** opened its doors in 1959 and remains a homely time warp, and **Louis Patisserie**, a tea room that opened in 1963 and hasn't changed its interior or the design for its cake boxes (created for its famous crèmes de marrons, gooey sweet chestnut purée layered with cream and sponge) since then. One final pit stop that even many locals don't know about, despite it being around for over forty years, is the **Antiques Emporium**, one of Hampstead's best kept secrets since 1967.

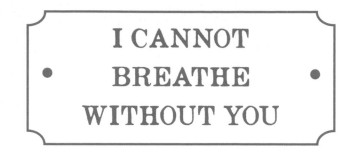

I CANNOT BREATHE WITHOUT YOU

So went the final words of one of John Keats' many love letters to Fanny Brawne, the tragic irony of a claim made only months before his tuberculosis became apparent. Keats met Fanny Brawne at Wentworth Place, where they lived in adjoining houses. While Fanny was 'coming out' into society, meeting dashing young officers from the Peninsular War, it was her mournful poet (his brother had died of consumption) that caught her eye and eventually her heart. The lovers became secretly engaged – Keats' poetry was no prospect as far as Fanny's mother was concerned – but the illicit couple were constantly torn apart due to Keats' illness and his trips to different parts of the country. The two would continue their desperately emotional correspondence, their frustration exacerbated by Fanny's ongoing social obligations on the arms of army officers. Strangely, it was the combination of jealousy and impending death that triggered the most productive period of Keats' poetic life. Back in Wentworth Place for the last time, Fanny was only allowed to visit Keats for very brief stints, for fear of making his condition worse; instead she would take walks past his window and the two sent each other a flurry of love notes. Even when the decision had been made to send Keats to Italy in one last bid to recover, Fanny's mother forbade the engagement; she did, however, promise that when he returned, he would marry Fanny and live with them. Perhaps she knew that months later, Keats would be dying in his friend's arms, weeping at the fact that he would never again see spring, the season he loved best. To his last breath, he kept writing, the one tangible consolation he had left.

CINDE-
RELLA

✤

C. S.
EVANS

A CHILD'S
GARDEN
OF VERSES

ROBERT
LOUIS
STEVENSON

CINDE-
RELLA

✤

C. S.
EVANS

FAR
FROM
THE
MADDING
CROWD

THOMAS
HARDY

EDWARD
LEAR

AN
ABC

ANNE
OF
GREEN
GABLES

✤

MONTGOMERY

LITTLE WOMEN
AND
GOOD WIVES

✤

LOUISA
MAY
ALCOTT

BORIS
PASTERNAK

✤

DOCTOR
ZHIVAGO

FROM RED LIGHTS
TO SILVER SCREENS

· ·

Shepherd Market

On the surface, **Shepherd Market** appears to be a genteel, village-like collection of restaurants, galleries and speciality shops, but lurking beneath is a far more salacious past. The warren of cobbled streets and overhanging buildings hosted, until 1708, the original 'May Fair' (from which the area takes its name) for fifteen days every May, before it was closed down for being too debauched. Until very recently, Shepherd Market was one of London's main red-light districts, and even now, as night falls, glimpses of a more upmarket industry can be seen in upstairs windows and through door cracks, with a number of escorts still at work. It is perhaps no surprise then that the Market was at the heart of one of this country's greatest political and sexual scandals (see **Stranger than Fiction**, overleaf).

Despite its shady past, today the shops lining the Market boast a fine selection of curiosities from the traditional to the contemporary: bookbinder **Sangorski & Sutcliffe** offers elegant and expensive special editions of classics and its own paper with delicate Japanese designs, and **Paul Thomas** is the florist for royal weddings and the Ritz.

It's not to be outdone on its 'boys' toys' either: if you are in the market for a genuine zebra-skin gun holder with blue suede lining, then **Anderson Wheeler** has an actual vault filled with guns and even a stuffed leopard; **Tradition of London Ltd** brings out the inner child, with its row upon row of miniature British Hussars that charge their Indian foe, sabres unsheathed and held high. Opposite the entrance to the Market, **Geo. F. Trumper** is known as the finest gentlemen's barber in London and continues to champion the lost art of shaving creams, soaps and brushes (perhaps to prepare for the allures within).

For dinner, Greta Garbo's favourite London restaurant, the tiny and very kitsch **L'Autre**, bizarrely mixes Polish and Mexican food. You won't find beetroot enchiladas on the menu though, as the two cuisines are thankfully kept apart.

The shadows of Mayfair's past float out of the Market and into its surrounding streets, well worth a post-dinner stroll – Half Moon Street is where the fictional Wooster of P. G. Wodehouse's novels lived; around the corner at 9 Curzon Place, Mama Cass of the Mamas and Papas died in July 1974 (allegedly choking on a sandwich in bed), and four years later, Keith Moon, drummer of The Who, overdosed in the very same bed. On Down Street, you can spot the entrance to what used to be Down Street station – during World War II, Churchill would often sleep down there, nicknaming it 'the Burrow', being one of the few places his ears were shielded from the noise of the Blitz.

Why, why is all so bright and gay?
There is no change, there is no cause;
My office-time I found to-day
Disgusting as it ever was.
At three, I went and tried the Clubs,
And yawned and saunter'd to and fro;
And now my heart jumps up and
  throbs,
And all my soul is in a glow.

Extract from 'The Mayfair Love-Song'
by William Makepeace Thackeray

For a final taste of a bygone era, walking through the doors of the **Curzon Mayfair** is like walking into 1950s Hollywood. Forget your jumbo Pepsi and pick 'n' mix; this picturehouse is about Pimm's in the summer and mulled wine in the winter, rubbing shoulders with people who dress up to watch the latest flick. It even has Royal Box seats if you're feeling particularly flush. Between 1951 and 1952, it was here that Max Ophüls' *La Ronde* was screened for a staggering seventeen months; seen by over half a million people, it reputedly brought about the introduction of the X certificate to the UK.

STRANGER THAN FICTION

On 8 September 1986, Lord Jeffrey Archer, multimillionaire novelist and member of Parliament, was alleged by the *Daily Star* to have paid for sex at Shepherd Market with Monica Coghlan. When the story was sold to a tabloid, Archer paid Coghlan £2,000 (now known in British slang as 'an Archer') to flee the country, and then sued the *Daily Star* for printing that he'd had sex with Coghlan for money. Thanks in large part to the impassioned and teary testimony of his wife (who allegedly was living a separate life to Archer at the time), he was cleared and the *Daily Star* ordered to pay damages.

However, over ten years later, as Archer was making a bid for the London mayoralty, a number of his friends came out of the woodwork to claim that they had created alibis for him at the time of the trial in return for money and the film rights to his future books (a promise he then reneged on). Archer was kicked out of the Tory party, but bounced back with a play he wrote, entitled *The Accused,* in which he played a prominent man defending himself in a court case, with the audience voting every night on whether he was guilty. That December, he was in court for real, facing charges of perjury, which he was eventually found guilty of and jailed. The final bizarre twist to the story is that, not long before the trial opened, Monica Coghlan, the girl from Shepherd Market, was killed in a drug-fuelled hit and run.

FROM SILK WEAVERS
TO DENNIS SEVERS

. . . .

Spitalfields

The nexus of Spitalfield streets – Princelet, Hanbury, Wilkes and Fournier – has housed a delicate balance of immigrant workers and genuine eastenders for over 300 years. Life from another era has, in some buildings, been preserved immaculately; in others, recreated or even fabricated. Peering through keyholes or shuttered windows, or even taking a tour inside these remarkable houses, the previous inhabitants seem to linger in the air.

What appear to be relics of a bygone era are literally scattered about the streets of Spitalfields – Roundells, or circular metal plates set into the pavement, each mysteriously engraved with a different emblem or image. Urban legend has it that these were set in the nineteenth century for the benefit of people who couldn't read. The truth is that a local sculptor was commissioned by the local council in the mid-1990s to cast them. Nevertheless, they represent the diverse history of Spitalfields: a weaver's shuttle and reels of thread in homage to London's silk-weaving community, brought over to Folgate Street by the French Huguenots in the 1720s (cast from a shuttle and reel found in Dennis Severs' house); the match girls from the Bryant & May factory who met in Hanbury Hall to create the first trade union; a henna-stencilled hand among the Bengali shops on Silk Street.

Fournier Street boasts probably the best collection of early Georgian townhouses in Britain, dating from the settlement of wealthy French Huguenots at the start of the eighteenth century. In Howard

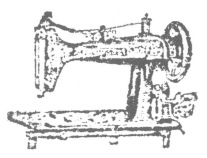

House at Number 14, the silk for Queen Victoria's Coronation gown was woven. But nowadays, it's become the destination street for modern conceptual artists, with trendsetters Tracey Emin and Gilbert & George among those responsible for restoring these exquisite houses to their Georgian splendour. The interior of Number 12 features in many of Gilbert & George's works, depicting the building in the 1970s as empty, dilapidated and gloomy.

Princelet Street was one of the first Spitalfield streets to be built, and two of its past inhabitants have been immortalised in their own unique way. In 1980 a room above the disused synagogue at **Number 19** was found abandoned, but left in its original state, down to porridge on the stove and the imprint of a head on a pillow. The occupant had been a young man, David Rodinsky, who simply vanished one day in the late 1960s. The artist Rachel Lichtenstein and East End chronicler Iain Sinclair went on a joint search for the man whom no one could describe or remember – a discomforting symbol for the ease with which people can slip through society's safety net. Their efforts are transcribed in the book *Rodinsky's Room*.

Number 13 is open all year round and can be booked for holidays or short stays – the housekeepers, Pat and Kathy, maintain the premises immaculately on behalf of the Landmark Trust, keeping the spirit of its original inhabitants alive and present. One can almost hear the weavers working away on the top floor, their babies asleep beneath their looms.

But the real jewel in the crown is **Dennis Severs' House** on Folgate Street. An eccentric Californian with unknown roots (see **The Man Behind the House**, overleaf), the late Dennis Severs created with painstaking detail and emotional depth the history and story of a completely fictional family, the Jervises, a Huguenot dynasty of silk-weavers. The concept behind the design is that the family have just popped out – leaving in their wake abandoned eggs in a mixing bowl on the kitchen table, a rumpled bed in the attic, an overturned chair in the drawing room. As a man with the wildest of imaginations but also an obsessive desire to evoke a sense of reality, Severs' attention to detail was so intricate that one vistor to the house became convinced that the Jervis family were her direct ancestors, culminating in a row with Severs and the woman in question being ejected.

For years, the cultural establishment sneered at Severs for prioritising this frolic of his imagination over historical accuracy, but his genius has now been roundly recognised, with the National Trust even sending curators to the building to learn about atmosphere. For it is this quality that Severs and the other guardians of the house relish above all else: visitors are instructed to remain absolutely silent throughout, for it is in the silence that the other senses are intensified and memory, the past and feelings of nostalgia rise to the fore. And to experience the house as Dennis Severs would have wanted it, every Monday night the house is candlelit. Even the candles have been strategically placed – in the kitchen, for example, a low candle on the table where the cook was studying a recipe book.

THE MAN BEHIND THE HOUSE

Captivated from an early age by the idea of 'Englishness', Dennis Severs first moved to London to run horse-drawn open carriage tours around Hyde Park; even then, the name of the tours, 'See Something Different Graciously', was indicative of how Severs saw the world. When he was evicted from his carriage house in South Kensington, the Queen, hearing of his plight, gave him emergency accommodation at the Royal Mews, where he acquired his first cat, Madge ('Her Majesty'). Severs' love of animals lasted his lifetime – generation after generation of Madges were doted upon along with budgies, which he would hang in cages on the shutters (as they did in the nineteenth century) until a kestrel savaged one through the bars; he even first arrived at Folgate Street in his horse-drawn carriage.

When Severs moved to the house in 1979, he slept in each of the ten rooms with a candle and chamberpot – his aim was not to restore, but to collect the soul of each room. Throughout the 1980s and '90s, he would regularly throw parties for his A-list friends in the upper rooms. His partner, Simon Pettet, was a craftsmen and tiler, able to recreate Delft tiles so authentically that they were indistinguishable from the seventeenth-century originals. The chimneypiece in Severs' bedroom is adorned with Pettet's tiles, each of them a portrait of Spitalfields residents and friends of the couple. They include a Tweedledee-and-Tweedledum-style picture of Gilbert & George and the depiction of a couple 'at it' in a Porsche, whose identity is legally hidden. Pettet died of Aids in December 1993; six years and a day later, Severs himself died, also of Aids.

LONDON THAT TIME FORGOT

Our selection of the best traditional and
vintage suppliers in the capital.

Paxton and Whitfield

93 Jermyn Street, SW1Y 6JE

Sir Winston Churchill once remarked,
'A gentleman only buys his cheese
from Paxton & Whitfield', and its
legacy as the finest cheesemonger in
the land continues today: the Royal
Family are among its distinguished
customers.

James Smith & Sons Umbrella Shop

53 New Oxford Street, WC1A 1BL

This world-famous establishment is a
work of art in itself. It first opened its
doors in the 1830s, and is still owned
and run as a family business. Smith &
Son's umbrellas, sticks and canes are
certainly not cheap, but are handmade
on site, and will last a lifetime.

Berry Brothers & Rudd

3 St James Street, SW1A 1EG

This Mayfair wine merchant is run by the eighth generation of the same family, has a subterranean wine school and even an underground tunnel which, although now blocked by wine racks, leads directly to St James's Palace. But the Brothers are definitely keeping up with the times, offering 'podcasks' on their website for wine lovers to download and listen to.

A. Gold

42 Brushfield Street, E1 6AG

Still bearing the sign of Amelia Gold's 1880 millinery, the shop is now home to a sumptuous array of traditional foods – from old favourites like Farrah's toffee and Scotch eggs, to lesser-known delights such as Earl Grey's Gingerbread Gentlemen and Mr Fitzpatrick's Blood Tonic Cordial. A. Gold is a feast for the eyes (and stomach).

F. Cooke's Pie and Mash Shop

9 Broadway Market, E8 4PH

A picture of current owner Bob Cooke with his pit bull hangs over the counter and surveys the Broadway Market institution that has been run by his family since 1900, and still serves up the same jellied eels, mashed spuds and liquor (parsley gravy), as it did back in the day.

Alfie's Antiques Market

13–25 Church Street, NW8

Less a market and more a department store spanning 35,000 feet and showcasing five centuries of jewellery, furniture, vintage posters and hundreds of other beautiful and rare objects. Alfie's has provided inspiration for designers including Jasper Conran and Kelly Hoppen. If you need a break from window shopping there is a charming café on the top floor.

L. Cornelissen & Son

. . . .

105 Great Russell Street, WC1B 3RY

Set up in the 1850s, this internationally renowned and enchanting artists' supply shop offers an array of brushes, calligraphy pens and inks, jars of pigments and pastels, gold leaf, oil paints and paper. They even supply the quills for period films.

Cecil Court

. . . .

Between Charing Cross Road and St Martin's Lane, WC2

Previously known as Flicker Alley after the concentration of early film companies in the Court, today it is a book lover's Mecca – the shopfronts have not been altered in more than a century and the traditional hanging signs announce specialists in rare and antiquarian books, maps and prints. There is even a fortune teller reading palms in the window of Watkins Books.

G. Baldwin & Co Pharmacy

. . . .

171–173 Walworth Road, SE17 1RW

An Aladdin's cave that has been selling herbal lotions, potions and remedies since 1844. Customers come to sip on pints of sarsaparilla while browsing its vast shelves for handmade soaps, herbal tinctures and even dragons' blood.

North Cross Vintage

. . . .

Fellbrigg Road, just off North Cross Road, SE22

A vintage emporium stuffed to the rafters with a cornucopia of books, signs, packaging, alpine sledges, woodblock lettering, door handles, greetings cards and more.

DIRECTORY and USEFUL ADDRESSES

LEAFY LONDON

From Swains Lane across Hampstead Heath

Kalendar Café
15a Swains Lane, N6 6QX
020 8348 8300

Parliament Hill Farmers' Market
William Ellis School, off Highgate Road, NW5 1RN
www.lfm.org.uk/markets/parliament-hill

Spring Fungi Foray
www.fungitobewith.org

Hampstead Ponds
Off Millfield Lane, N6

Kenwood House
Hampstead Lane, NW3 7JR
020 8348 1286
www.english-heritage.org.uk/daysout/properties/kenwood-house

Pergola and Hill Garden
Inverforth Close, off North End Way, NW3 7EX
020 7332 3322

Wells Pub
30 Well Walk, NW3 1BX
020 7794 3785
www.thewellshampstead.co.uk

From Fairy Tales to Flamingoes
Kensington Gardens

Serpentine Lido
www.serpentinelido.com

Serpentine Gallery
Kensington Gardens, W2 3XA
020 7402 6075
www.serpentinegallery.org

Kensington Palace
Kensington Gardens, W84 PX
020 3166 6000
www.hrp.org.uk/KensingtonPalace

Albert Memorial
Kensington Gardens,
Kensington Gore, SW7
020 7298 2100
www.royalparks.org.uk/parks/kensington-gardens

Kensington Roof Gardens
99 Kensington High Street, W8 5SA
020 7368 3993
www.roofgardens.virgin.com

From the Isabella Plantation to Petersham Nurseries
Richmond Park

Richmond Terrace Gardens
Richmond, TW10 6RH

Isabella Plantation

Richmond Park, TW10 5HS
020 8948 3209
www.royalparks.org.uk/parks/richmond-park/isabella-plantation.cfm

Kingston Riding Centre

38 Crescent Road, KT2 7RG
020 8546 6361
www.kingstonridingcentre.com

Kitevibe

07866 430979
www.kitevibe.com

Chez Lindsay

11 Hill Rise, TW10 6UQ
020 8948 7473
www.chez-lindsay.co.uk

Petersham Nurseries

Church Lane & Petersham Road, TW10 7AG
020 8940 5230
www.petershamnurseries.com

From Portraits to Pelicans
St James's Park

St James's Park

St James's Park, Horse Guards Road, SW1A 2BJ
www.royalparks.org.uk/parks/st-jamess-park

National Gallery

Trafalgar Square, WC2N 5DN
020 7747 2885
www.nationalgallery.org.uk

National Portrait Gallery

2 St Martin's Place, WC2H 0HE
020 7306 0055
www.npg.org.uk

Institute of Contemporary Arts

The Mall, SW1Y 5AH
020 7930 3647
www.ica.org.uk

Buckingham Palace

Buckingham Palace, SW1A 1AA
020 7930 4832
www.royal.gov.uk

Inn the Park

St James's Park, Horse Guards Road, SW1A 2BJ
020 7451 9999
www.innthepark.com

Trafalgar Hotel

2 Spring Gardens, Trafalgar Square, SW1A 2TS
020 7870 2900
www.thetrafalgar.com

Gordon's Wine Bar

47 Villiers Street, Embankment, WC2N 6NE
020 7930 1408
www.gordonswinebar.com

LATE-NIGHT LONDON

• • • • • • • • • • • • • • • • • • •

From Kingsland Road to Ridley Road *Dalston*

A Little of What You Fancy

464 Kingsland Road, E8 4AE
020 7275 0060
www.alittleofwhatyoufancy.info

Arcola Theatre

24 Ashwin Street, E8 3DL
020 7503 1646
www.arcolatheatre.com

Café Oto

18–22 Ashwin Street, E8 3DL
020 7923 1231
www.caféoto.co.uk

Dalston Roof Park

Bootstrap Company
The Print House, 18 Ashwin Street, E8 3DL
www.bootstrapcompany.co.uk/13_dalston_roof_park

Dalston Jazz Bar
4 Bradbury Street, N16 8JN
020 7254 9728

Vortex Jazz Club
11 Gillett Square, N16 8AZ
020 7254 4097
www.vortexjazz.co.uk

Mangal Ocakbasi Restaurant
10 Arcola Street, E8 2DJ
020 7275 8981
www.mangal1.com

Efes Pool Club and Bar
17 Stoke Newington Road, N16 8BH
020 7249 6040

Ridley Road Market Bar
49 Ridley Road, E8 2NP
www.facebook.com/ridleyroad

Rio Cinema
107 Kingsland High Street, E8 2PB
020 7241 9410
www.riocinema.org.uk

Dalston Superstore
117 Kingsland High Street, E8 2PB
020 7254 2273
www.dalstonsuperstore.com

The Alibi
91 Kingsland High Street, E8 2PB
020 7249 2733
www.thealibilondon.co.uk

The Nest
36 Stoke Newington Road, N16 7XJ
020 7354 9993
www.ilovethenest.com

From Exmouth Market to Lucky Voice *Islington*

Exmouth Market
Clerkenwell, EC1R 4QL
www.exmouthmarket.co.uk

Dollar Bar and Grill
2 Exmouth Market, EC1R 4PX
020 7278 0077
www.dollargrillsandmartinis.com

Café Kick
43 Exmouth Market, EC1R 4QL
020 7837 8077
www.cafekick.co.uk

Morito
32 Exmouth Market, EC1R 4QE
020 7278 7007
www.morito.co.uk

Caravan
11–13 Exmouth Market, EC1R 4QD
020 7833 8115
www.caravanonexmouth.co.uk

The Family Business
58 Exmouth Market, EC1R 4QE
020 7278 9526
www.thefamilybusinesstattoo.com

Sadler's Wells
Rosebery Avenue, EC1R 4TN
020 7863 8198
www.sadlerswells.com

Charles Lamb
16 Elia Street, N1 8DE
020 7837 5040
www.thecharleslambpub.com

69 Colebrooke Row
N1 8AA
07540 528593
www.69colebrookerow.com

Camden Passage
Islington, N1 8FA
www.camdenpassageislington.co.uk

The Elk in the Woods
37–39 Camden Passage, N1 8EA
020 7226 3535
www.the-elk-in-the-woods.co.uk

Almeida Theatre
Almeida Street, N1 1TA
020 7359 4404
www.almeida.co.uk

King's Head Theatre
115 Upper Street, N1 1QN
020 3286 8788
www.kingsheadtheatre.org

Lucky Voice
173–174 Upper Street, N1 1RG
020 7354 6280
www.luckyvoice.com

Public House
54 Islington Park Street, N1 1PX
020 7359 6070
www.boutiquepubs.com

From Great Windmill Street to Dean Street *The Seven Noses of Soho*

Mark's Bar
66 Brewer Street, W1F 9UP
020 7292 3518
www.marksbar.co.uk

Criterion Theatre
2 Jermyn Street, SW1Y 4XA
020 7839 8811
www.criterion-theatre.co.uk

Admiralty Arch
The Mall, SW1A 2WH
020 7276 1800

Heliot
The Hippodrome Casino, 10–14 Cranbourn Street,
WC2H 7JH
020 7769 8844
www.hippodromecasino.com/heliot

Circus
27–29 Endell Street, WC2H 9BA
020 7420 9300
www.circus-london.co.uk

Da Mario
63 Endell Street, WC2H 9AJ
020 7240 3632
www.da-mario.co.uk

Copita
26–27 D'Arblay Street, W1F 8EL
020 7287 7797
www.copita.co.uk

Milk Bar
3 Bateman Street, W1D 4AG
020 7287 4796

Ronnie Scott's
47 Frith Street, W1D 4HT
020 7439 0747
www.ronniescotts.co.uk

Soho Theatre
21 Dean Street, W1D 3NE
020 7478 0100
www.sohotheatre.com

Dean Street Townhouse
69–71 Dean Street, W1D 3SE
020 7434 1775
www.deanstreettownhouse.com

From First Thursdays to Last Orders *Shoreditch*

First Thursdays
Whitechapel Gallery
77–82 Whitechapel High Street, E1 7QX
020 7522 7888
www.firstthursdays.co.uk

Ninetyeight Bar & Lounge
98 Curtain Road, EC2A 3AF
0207 729 0087
www.ninetyeight-bar-lounge.com

Vintage Emporium
14 Bacon Street, E1 6LF
020 7739 0799
www.vintageemporiumcafé.com

Callooh Callay
65 Rivington Street, EC2A 3AY
020 7739 4781
www.calloohcallaybar.com

Cay Tre
301 Old Street, EC1V 9LA
020 7729 8662
www.vietnamesekitchen.co.uk/caytre

Rivington Bar and Grill
38-40 Rivington Street, EC2A 3DG
020 7729 7053
www.rivingtonshoreditch.co.uk

Pizza East
56 Shoreditch High Street, E1 6JJ
020 7729 1888
www.pizzaeast.com

Concrete
Lower Ground Floor, 56 Shoreditch High Street, E1 6JJ
020 7729 1888
www.concretespace.co.uk

The Book Club
100–106 Leonard Street, EC2A 4RH
020 7684 8618
www.wearetbc.com

Shoreditch Town Hall
380 Old Street, EC1V 9LT
020 7739 6176
www.shoreditchtownhall.org.uk

Rich Mix
35–47 Bethnal Green Road, E1 6LA
020 7613 7498
www.richmix.org.uk

Queen of Hoxton
1–5 Curtain Road, EC2A 3JX
020 7422 0958
www.queenofhoxton.com

Nightjar
129 City Road, EC1V 1JB
020 7253 4101
www.barnightjar.com

LAST-MINUTE LONDON

• • • • • • • • • • • • • • • • • • • •

From Buenos Aires to East India
Greenwich

Docklands Light Railway
www.dlrlondon.co.uk

Buenos Aires Café
86 Royal Hill, SE10 8RT
020 8488 6764
www.buenosairesltd.com/bac-green.html

Royal Observatory
Blackheath Avenue, SE10 8XJ
020 8858 6565
www.rmg.co.uk/royal-observatory

Old Royal Naval College
King William Walk, SE10 9NN
020 8269 4799
www.ornc.org

Biscuit Ceramic Café
3–4 Nelson Road, SE10 9JB
020 8853 8588
www.biscuit-biscuit.com

Greenwich Market
College Approach, SE10 9HZ
www.shopgreenwich.co.uk/greenwich-market

Greenwich foot tunnel
Cutty Sark Gardens, SE10 9HT
www.royalgreenwich.gov.uk/Greenwich/LeisureCulture/
Architecture/GreenwichFootTunnel.htm

Island Gardens Park
Saunders Ness Road, E14 3EB

Mudchute Park and Farm
Pier Street, E14 3HP
020 7515 5901
www.mudchute.org

The Gun
27 Coldharbour, Docklands, E14 9NS
020 7515 5222
www.thegundocklands.com

Fatboy's Diner
Trinity Buoy Wharf, 64 Orchard Place, E14 0JW
020 7987 4334
www.fatboysdiner.co.uk

From Hungerford Bridge to Oxo Tower *The South Bank*

National Theatre
South Bank, SE1 9PX
020 7452 3600
www.nationaltheatre.org.uk

Royal Festival Hall
Southbank Centre, Belvedere Road, SE1 8XX
020 7960 4200
www.southbankcentre.co.uk/venues/royal-festival-hall

London Eye
Minster Court, SE1 7JB
0870 990 8881
www.londoneye.com

Southbank Centre
(See details for Royal Festival Hall)

Saison Poetry Library
Level 5, Royal Festival Hall, SE1 8XX
020 7921 0943/0664
www.poetrylibrary.org.uk

Southbank book market
Belvedere Road, SE1 7GA

Oxo Tower
Oxo Tower Wharf, Barge House Street, SE1 9PH
020 7803 3888
www.harveynichols.com/oxo-tower-london

Anchor & Hope
36 The Cut, SE1 8LP
020 7928 9898

From Maltby Street to Southwark Cathedral *Bermondsey*

Borough Market
151 Borough High Street, SE1 1HR
020 7407 1002
www.boroughmarket.org.uk

St John Bakery
Arch 72, Druid Street, SE1 2DU
020 7237 5999
www.stjohnbakerycompany.com

Southwark Cathedral
London Bridge, SE1 9DA
020 7367 6700
www.cathedral.southwark.anglican.org

Shakespeare's Globe
21 New Globe Walk, SE1 9DT
020 7902 1400
www.shakespearesglobe.com

Rose Theatre
56 Park Street, SE1 9AS
020 7261 9565
www.rosetheatre.org.uk

HMS Belfast
The Queen's Walk, SE1 2JH
020 7940 6300
www.hmsbelfast.iwm.org.uk

Blueprint Café
1st Floor, Design Museum, 28 Shad Thames, SE1 2YD
020 7378 7031
www.blueprintcafe.co.uk

The Mayflower
117 Rotherhithe Street, SE16 4NF
020 7237 4088
www.themayflowerrotherhithe.com

José
104 Bermondsey Street, SE1 3UB
020 7403 4902
www.joserestaurant.co.uk

Pizarro
194 Bermondsey Street, SE1 3TQ
020 7407 7339
www.josepizarro.com/restaurants/pizarro

M.Manze
87 Tower Bridge Road, SE1 4TW
020 7277 6181
www.manze.co.uk

Magdalen
152 Tooley Street, SE1 2TU
020 7403 1342
www.magdalenrestaurant.co.uk

Holly and Lil
103 Bermondsey Street, SE1 3XB
020 3287 3024
www.hollyandlil.co.uk

The Garrison
99 Bermondsey Street, SE1 3XB
020 7089 9355
www.thegarrison.co.uk

Shortwave Cinema
10 Bermondsey Square, SE1 3UN
020 7357 6845
www.shortwavefilms.co.uk

Six Wines Eight
10 Bermondsey Square, SE1 3UN
020 7357 6845
www.sixwineseight.com

From Salt Beef on Rye to Great Balls of Fire *Brick Lane*

Brick Lane Mosque
59 Brick Lane, E1 6QL
020 7247 6052
www.bricklanejammemasjid.co.uk

Beigel Bake
159 Brick Lane, E1 6SB
020 7729 0616

The Carpenter's Arms
73 Cheshire Street, E2 6EG
020 7739 6342
www.carpentersarmsfreehouse.com

Old Truman Brewery
91 Brick Lane, E1 6QL
020 7770 6000
www.trumanbrewery.com

93 Feet East
150 Brick Lane, E1 6QL
020 7770 6006
www.93feeteast.co.uk

All Star Lanes
95 Brick Lane, E1 6QL
020 7426 9200
www.allstarlanes.co.uk/venues/brick-lane

Preem
124 Brick Lane, E1 6RU
020 7247 0397
www.preemprithi.co.uk

Aladin
132 Brick Lane, E1 6RU
020 7247 8210
www.aladinbricklane.co.uk

Old Spitalfields Market
Brushfield Street, E1 6AA
020 7247 8556
www.oldspitalfieldsmarket.com

St John Bread and Wine
94–96 Commercial Street, E1 6LZ
020 3301 8069
www.stjohngroup.uk.com

Montezuma's
51 Brushfield Street, E1 6AA
020 7539 9208
www.montezumas.co.uk

The Golden Heart
110 Commercial Street, E1 6LZ
020 7247 2158

Des and Lorraine's Junk Shop
14 Bacon Street, E1 6LF

LAZY LONDON

• • • • • • • • • • • • • • • • • •

From Caged Birds to Potted Pigs
Columbia Road

Columbia Road Flower Market
Columbia Road, E2
www.columbiaroad.info

The Birdcage
80 Columbia Road, E2 7QB

Seamus Ryan's Sunday Shoots
7 Ezra Street, E2 7RH
020 7613 1560
www.sundayshoots.com

Ryantown
126 Columbia Road, E2 7RG
020 7613 1510
www.ryantownshop.blogspot.co.uk

Suck and Chew
130 Columbia Road, E2 7RG
www.suckandchew.co.uk

Three Letter Man
146a Columbia Road, E2 7RG
www.threeletterman.com

Printers and Stationers
21a Ezra Street, E2 7RH
020 7729 9496
www.printersandstationers.co.uk

Brawn
49 Columbia Road, E2 7RG
020 7729 5692
www.brawn.com

Jones' Dairy
23 Ezra Street, E2 7RH
www.jonesdairy.co.uk

Campania Gastronomia
95 Columbia Road, E2 7RG
020 7613 0015

Goldsmith Row book market
Goldsmith Row, E2
www.goldsmithrowbookmarket.com

From Hugo's to Lexi's
Queen's Park and Kensal Rise

Hugo's
25 Lonsdale Road, NW6 6RA
020 7372 1232
www.hugosrestaurant.co.uk

Queen's Park Farmers' Market
Salusbury Road Primary School, Salusbury Road, NW6 6RG
www.lfm.org.uk/markets/queens-park

The Salusbury
50–52 Salusbury Road, NW6 6NN
020 7328 3286
www.thesalusbury.co.uk

Iris
73 Salusbury Road, NW6 6NJ
020 7372 1777
www.irisfashion.co.uk

Queen's Park Books
87 Salusbury Road, NW6 6NH
020 7625 1008
www.queensparkbooks.co.uk

Kensal Green Cemetery
Harrow Road, W10 4RA
www.kensalgreencemetery.com

Paradise by Way of Kensal Green
19 Kilburn Lane, W10 4AE
020 8969 0098
www.theparadise.co.uk

Ida
167 Fifth Avenue, W10 4DL
020 8969 9853
www.idarestaurant.co.uk

The Shop
75 Chamberlayne Road, NW10 3ND
020 8969 9399

Scarlet and Violet
76 Chamberlayne Road, NW10 3JJ
020 8969 9446
www.scarletandviolet.com

The Lexi
194b Chamberlayne Road, NW10 3JU
0871 704 2069
www.thelexicinema.co.uk

From Afternoon Picnics to Twilight Barking

La Petite Poissonerie
75 Gloucester Avenue, NW1 8LD
020 7483 4435
www.lapetite-poissonerie.co.uk

Melrose and Morgan
42 Gloucester Avenue, NW1 8JD
020 7722 0011
www.melroseandmorgan.com

Primrose Hill Bakery
69 Gloucester Avenue, NW1 8LD
020 7483 4222
www.primrosebakery.org.uk

Yeomans greengrocers
152 Regent's Park Road, NW1 8XN

St Mary's
The Parish Church of St Mary the Virgin
Elsworthy Road, NW3 3DJ
020 7722 3238
www.stmarysprimrosehill.com

TriYoga
6 Erskine Road, NW3 3AJ
020 7483 3344
www.triyoga.co.uk

Manna
4 Erskine Road, NW3 3AJ
020 7722 8028
www.mannav.com

The Engineer
65 Gloucester Avenue, NW1 8JH
020 7483 1890
www.theengineerprimrosehill.co.uk

Queens
49 Regent's Park Road, NW1 8XD
Tel: 020 7586 0408
www.thequeensprimrosehill.co.uk

Odette
130 Regent's Park Road, NW1 8XL
020 7586 8569
www.odettesprimrosehill.com

Lemonia
89 Regent's Park Road, NW1 8UY
Tel: 020 7586 7454
www.lemonia.co.uk

Trojka
101 Regent's Park Road, NW1 8UR
Tel: 020 7483 3765
www.trojka.co.uk

From Dressing Gowns to Beach Blankets *Notting Hill*

Portobello Road Market
Portobello Road, W11 1LJ
020 7229 8354
www.portobelloroad.co.uk

What Katie Did
26 Portobello Green, 281 Portobello Road, W10 5TZ
0845 430 8943
www.whatkatiedid.com

Ollie & Bow
69 Golborne Road, W10 5NP
07768 790725

Les Couilles du Chien
65 Golborne Road, W10 5NP
020 8968 0099
www.lescouillesduchien.com

Kokon to Zai
86 Golborne Road, W10 5PS
020 8960 3736
www.kokontozai.co.uk

The Electric
191 Portobello Road, W11 2ED
020 7908 9696
www.electriccinema.co.uk

Chaya Teahouse
14a Saint Luke's Road, W11 1DP
020 7243 0374
www.teanamu.com/teahouse

Brora
187 Westbourne Grove, W11 2SB
020 7229 1515
www.brora.co.uk

Aesop
227a Westbourne Grove, W11 2SE
020 7221 2008
www.aesop.com

Tom's Deli
226 Westbourne Grove, W11 2RH
020 7221 8818
www.tomsdeli.co.uk

Daylesford Organic
208–212 Westbourne Grove, W11 2RH
020 7313 8050
www.daylesfordorganic.com

Porchester Spa
The Porchester Centre, Queensway, W2 5HS
020 7792 3980
www.better.org.uk/leisure/porchester-spa

Beach Blanket Babylon
45 Ledbury Road, W11 2AA
020 7229 2907
www.beachblanket.co.uk

The Print Room
34 Hereford Road, W2 5AJ
020 7221 6036
www.the-print-room.org

Inaho
4 Hereford Road, W2 4AA
020 7221 8495

LEARNED LONDON

• • • • • • • • • • • • • • • • • • •

From Gauguin's Nude to Freud's Ice Cream *Somerset House and Aldwych*

Somerset House
Strand, WC2R 1LA
020 7845 4600
www.somersethouse.org.uk

Courtauld Gallery
Somerset House, Strand, WC2R 0RN
020 7872 0220
www.courtauld.ac.uk/gallery

Art History Tours
www.arthistoryuk.com

American Bar
Savoy Hotel, Strand, WC2R 0EU
020 7836 4343
www.fairmont.com/savoy-london

The Delaunay
55 Aldwych, WC2B 4BB
020 7499 8558
www.thedelaunay.com

From Irish Giants to Bleeding Hearts *Lincoln's Inn Fields*

Lincoln's Inn Fields
Newman's Row, WC2A 3TL
020 7405 1393
www.lincolnsinn.org.uk

Hunterian Museum
The Royal College of Surgeons of England
35–43 Lincoln's Inn Fields, WC2A 3PE
020 7869 6560
www.rcseng.ac.uk/museums

Sir John Soane's Museum
13 Lincoln's Inn Fields, WC2A 3BP
020 7405 2107
www.soane.org

32 Great Queen Street
WC2B 5AA
020 7242 0622

Bleeding Heart Yard
19 Greville Street, EC1N 8SJ
020 7242 2056/8238
www.bleedingheart.co.uk

From the Literary Letter Writer to the Botanical Pornographer *Chelsea*

Carlyle's House
24 Cheyne Row, SW3 5HL
020 7352 7087
www.nationaltrust.org.uk/carlyles-house

Chelsea Physic Garden
66 Royal Hospital Road, SW3 4HS
020 7352 5646
www.chelseaphysicgarden.co.uk

Cheyne Walk Brasserie
50 Cheyne Walk, SW3 5LR
020 7376 8787
www.cheynewalkbrasserie.com

From Dulwich Picture Gallery to the Horniman Museum *Dulwich and Forest Hill*

Dulwich Picture Gallery
Gallery Road, SE21 7AD
020 8693 5254
www.dulwichpicturegallery.org.uk

Beauberry House
Gallery Road, SE21 7AB
020 8299 9788
www.beauberryhouse.co.uk

London Recumbents
Ranger's Yard, Dulwich Park, College Road, SE21 7BQ
020 8299 6636
www.londonrecumbents.com

Horniman Museum
100 London Road, SE23 3PQ
020 8699 1872
www.horniman.ac.uk

LIVE LONDON

● ● ● ● ● ● ● ● ● ● ● ● ● ● ● ● ● ● ● ●

From London Zoo to Open Air Theatre *Regent's Park*

Camden Market
Camden High Street & Chalk Farm Road, NW1 8AH
www.camden-market.org

London Zoo
Regent's Park, NW1 4RY
020 7722 3333
www.zsl.org/zsl-london-zoo

Queen Mary's Rose Garden
Regent's Park, NW1 4NR
020 7486 7905
www.royalparks.org.uk/parks/the-regents-park

The Honest Sausage
Regent's Park, The Broadwalk, NW1 4NU
www.companyofcooks.com/locations/our-locations/
honest-sausage

Regent's Park Open Air Theatre
Inner Circle, Regent's Park, NW1 4NU
0844 826 4242
www.openairtheatre.org

Canal Café Theatre
Delamere Terrace, W2 6ND
020 7209 6054
www.canalcafétheatre.com

From Public Houses to Music Halls *Wapping*

Prospect of Whitby
57 Wapping Wall, E1W 3SH
020 7481 1095
www.taylor-walker.co.uk/pub/prospect-of-whitby-
wapping/c8166

Wapping Project
Wapping Hydraulic Power Station, E1W 3SG
020 7680 2080
www.thewappingproject.com

The Wapping Project Bookshop
Wapping Hydraulic Power Station, E1W 3SG
020 7680 2080
www.wappingprojectbookshop.com

Wilton's Music Hall
1 Graces Alley, E1 8JB
020 7702 9555
www.wiltons.org.uk

From Brockwell Park to The Brixton Academy *Brixton*

Brockwell Park
Norwood Road, SE24 0PA
020 7926 9000
www.brockwellpark.com

Brixton Windmill
Windmill Gardens, West end of Blenheim Gardens,
Off Brixton Hill, SW2 5EU
020 7926 6213
www.brixtonwindmill.org

Brixton Market
Electric Avenue, SW9 8JX
07960 942060
www.brixtonmarket.net

Brixi
Unit 7, Second Avenue, Brixton Village, SW9 8PR
07919 162428

WAGfree
26 Brixton Village, SW9 8PR
020 7274 6267
www.wagfreefood.com

Honest Burgers
Unit 12, Brixton Village, SW9 8PR
020 7733 7963
www.honestburgers.co.uk

LAB G
6 Granville Arcade, Coldharbour Lane, SW9 8PR
07803 922616

Brixton Academy
211 Stockwell Road, SW9 9SL
020 7771 3000
www.o2academybrixton.co.uk

Hootananny
95 Effra Road, SW2 1DF
020 7737 7273
www.hootanannybrixton.co.uk

The Effra
38a Kellet Road, SW2 1EB
020 7274 4180

Fujiyama
5–7 Vining Street, SW9 8QA
020 7737 2369
www.newfujiyama.com

Upstairs
89b Acre Lane (entrance on Branksome Road), SW2 5TN
0207 733 8855
www.upstairslondon.com

From Culture to Sculpture
King's Cross

Kings Place
90 York Way, N1 9AG
020 7520 1490
www.kingsplace.co.uk

The School of Life
70 Marchmont Street, WC1N 1AB
020 7833 1010
www.theschooloflife.com

St Pancras Champagne Bar
St Pancras International, Upper Concourse,
Euston Road, N1C 4QL
0207 870 9900
www.searcyschampagnebars.co.uk/st-pancras-grand-home.php

St Pancras Hotel
Euston Road, NW1 2AR
020 7841 3540
www.marriott.co.uk/hotels/travel/lonpr-st-pancras

06 St Chad's Place
WC1X 9HH
020 7278 3355
www.6stchadsplace.com

LEFT-FIELD LONDON
• • • • • • • • • • • • • • • • • • •

From Dinosaurs to Leather Jackets
Crystal Palace

Crystal Palace Gardens
Thicket Road, SE20 8DT
www.gardenvisit.com/garden/crystal_palace_park

Crystal Palace Museum
Anerley Hill, SE19 2BA
020 8676 0700
www.crystalpalacemuseum.org.uk

Bambino
32 Church Road, SE19 2ET
07956 323164
www.facebook.com/BambinoVolcano

Antiques Warehouse
Imperial House, Jasper Road, SE19 1SG
020 8480 7042
www.crystalpalaceantiques.com

Exhibition Rooms
69–71 Westow Hill, SE19 1TX
020 8761 1175
www.theexhibitionrooms.com

From Eel Pie Island to Strawberry Hill *Twickenham*

Eel Pie Island art studios
Eel Pie Island, TW1 3DY
www.eelpieislandartists.co.uk

Ripple
Eel Pie Island, TW1 3DY
www.vrbo.com/308994

The Fox
39 Church Street, TW1 3NR
020 8892 1535
www.thefoxpubtwickenham.co.uk

Strawberry Hill House
268 Waldegrave Road, TW1 4ST
020 8744 1241
www.strawberryhillhouse.org.uk

From Lauderdale to Laudanum *Highgate Cemetery*

Lauderdale House
Waterlow Park, Highgate Hill, N6 5HG
020 8348 8716
www.lauderdalehouse.co.uk

Waterlow Park
Dartmouth Park Hill, N19 5JF
www.waterlowpark.org.uk

Highgate Cemetery
Swain's Lane, N6 6PJ
020 8340 1834
www.highgate-cemetery.org

The Flask
77 Highgate West Hill, N6 6BU
020 8348 7346
www.theflaskhighgate.com

From the Hackney Pearl to the Olympic Park *Hackney Wick*

Scrap Club
www.scrapclub.co.uk

Films on Fridges
Forman Smokehouse Gallery Yard, Stour Road, E3 2NT
www.filmsonfridges.com

The Hackney Pearl
11 Prince Edward Road, E9 5LX
020 8510 3605
www.thehackneypearl.com

Flea Market
White Post Lane, E9 5EN
www.hw-fm.tumblr.com

Broadway Market
E8 4PH
07872 463409
www.broadwaymarket.co.uk

Yard Theatre
Queen's Yard, E9 5EN
www.theyardtheatre.co.uk

Elevator Gallery
Mother Studios, Queen's Yard, White Post Lane, E9 5EN
07849 651993
www.elevatorgallery.co.uk

Stour Space
7 Roach Road, E3 2PA
020 8985 7827
www.stourspace.co.uk

Counter Café
7 Roach Road, E3 2PA
07834 275 920
www.thecountercafé.co.uk

H. Forman & Son
Stour Road, E3 2NT
020 8525 2399
www.formans.co.uk

LOST LONDON

• • • • • • • • • • • • • • • • • • •

From Towering Monuments to Ancient Ruins *The City of London*

Monument
Fish Street Hill, EC3R 6DB
020 7626 2717
www.themonument.info

Leadenhall Market
Gracechurch Street, EC3V 1LR
www.leadenhallmarket.co.uk

Jamaica Wine House
St Michael's Alley, EC3V 9DS
020 7929 6972
www.jamaicawinehouse.co.uk

The Royal Exchange
Bank, EC3V 3LR
020 7621 0077
www.theroyalexchange.com

No. 1 Poultry and Coq d'Argent
EC2R 8JR
020 7395 5000
www.coqdargent.co.uk

Church of St Stephen Walbrook
39 Walbrook, EC4N 8BN
020 7626 9000
www.ststephenwalbrook.net

Temple of Mithras
Walbrook Street, EC4N
0871 961 1823

Guildhall
Gresham Street, EC2V 7HH
020 7332 1313
www.guildhall.cityoflondon.gov.uk

St Paul's Cathedral
St Paul's Churchyard, EC4M 8AD
020 7236 8350
www.stpauls.co.uk

St Bartholomew the Great
West Smithfield, EC1A 9DS
020 7606 5171
www.greatstbarts.com

From the **1690**s to the **1960**s *Hampstead*

Fenton House
Hampstead Grove, NW3 6SP
020 7435 3471
www.nationaltrust.org.uk/fenton-house

Burgh House
New End Square, NW3 1LT
020 7431 0144
www.burghhouse.org.uk

Keats House
Keats Grove, NW3
020 7332 3868
www.keatshouse.cityoflondon.gov.uk

2 Willow Road
NW3 1TH
www.nationaltrust.org.uk/2-willow-road

The Coffee Cup
74 Hampstead High Street, NW3 1QX
020 7435 7565
www.coffeecupuk.com

Le Cellier du Midi
28 Church Row, NW3 6UP
020 7435 9998
www.lecellierdumidi.com

Louis Patisserie
32 Heath Street, NW3 6TE
020 7435 9908

Antiques Emporium
12 Heath Street, NW3 6TE
020 7794 3297
www.hampsteadantiqueemporium.co.uk

From Red Lights to Silver Screens
Shepherd Market

Shepherd Market
Westminster, W1J 7PH
www.shepherdmarket.co.uk

Sangorski & Sutcliffe
46 Curzon Street, W1J 7UH
www.bookbinding.co.uk/Sangorski.htm

Paul Thomas
4 Shepherd Street, W1J 7JD
020 7499 6889
www.paulthomasflowers.co.uk

Anderson Wheeler
13 Shepherd Market, W1J 7PQ
020 7499 9315
www.andersonwheeler.co.uk

Tradition of London Ltd
5a Shepherd Street, W1J 7HW
020 7493 7452
www.traditionoflondon.com

Geo. F. Trumper
9 Curzon Street, W1J 5HQ
020 7499 1850
www.trumpers.com

L'Autre
5b Shepherd Street, W1J 7HP
020 7499 4680

Curzon Mayfair
38 Curzon Street, W1J 7TY
0330 500 1331
www.curzoncinemas.com/cinemas/mayfair

From Silk Weavers to Dennis Severs *Spitalfields*

19 Princelet Street
19 Princelet Street, E1 6QH
020 7247 5352
www.19princeletstreet.org.uk

13 Princelet Street
E1 6QH
www.landmarktrust.org.uk/BuildingDetails/
Overview/235/Princelet_Street

Dennis Severs' House
18 Folgate Street, E1 6BX
020 7247 4013
www.dennissevershouse.co.uk

ACKNOWLEDGEMENTS

· ·

We would like to thank Candice Baseden,
Alice Brett, Felicity Blunt, William Charrington,
Julia Connolly, Rosemary Davidson, Sara Foster,
Ian Goodman, Tara Hacking, Kristen Harrison,
Laura Hassan, Bea Hodgkin, Laura Holmes,
Beth Housdon, Ilona Jasiewicz, Tom Marks,
Ben Murphy, Molly Oldfield, Catherine Phillips,
Flo Phillips, Rowan Powell, Rebecca Ritchie,
Simon Rhodes, Anya Rosenberg, The Aardvarks-
on-sea: Lesley and Pea, Andrea Vickers, Adrian Vickers,
Emma Vickers, Matt Vickers, Vanessa Webb
and Hannah Westland.

Permission to quote Leonard Woolf, p164, with
thanks to the University of Sussex and Society
of Authors as the Estate of Leonard Woolf.

Permission to quote from John Betjeman's
'Cornish Cliffs', with thanks to John Murray.

Sophie and Sam

INDEX

• •

Page numbers in *italics* indicate photographs.

LIST OF IMAGES

• •

FOR MAPS AND MORE VISIT

· ·

www.londonforlovers.net

· ·

FOLLOW US ON TWITTER

@London4Lovers